PIRATES & PRIVATEERS

—— *from* ——

LONG ISLAND SOUND
to DELAWARE BAY

JAMIE L.H. GOODALL

THE
History
PRESS

Published by The History Press
Charleston, SC
www.historypress.com

First published 2022

ISBN 978-1-54025-203-6

Library of Congress Control Number: 2022931448

To those who believed I could.

Will Turner: This is either madness or brilliance.
Jack Sparrow: It's remarkable how often those two traits coincide.
—Pirates of the Caribbean

CONTENTS

CONTENTS

ACKNOWLEDGEMENTS

W hen writing a book, it can often feel like an isolating venture; just you, the archival material and your words—just you, the computer and the auto-save function you hoped you remembered to activate. But the creation of a book is truly built in community. Such an endeavor necessitates technical, editorial and moral support. I am immensely grateful to my editor, Kate Jenkins; my copy editor, Ashley Hill; and those at The History Press who decided working with me again wouldn't be too terrible! Their support made the process of producing a second book as painless as possible. I also owe a great debt of gratitude to the team at the Institute of Historical Research: School of Advanced Study University of London. Their no doubt tireless work transcribing forty-one volumes of records contained in the *Calendar of State Papers, America and the West Indies* and making these records freely available on British History Online were critical to the foundation of this book. Without those records, this book could not exist. And a special shout-out to the institutions whose open-access resources enabled me to incorporate the fantastic images you see within these pages: the Library of Congress, the Metropolitan Museum of Art and Wikimedia Commons.

I would also like to share my appreciation for the giants who came before me, the scholars whose contributions to the historical profession provided me with a purpose and direction. A sincere thank-you is also due to my Twittersphere, especially all the Twitterstorians, my followers, my History Ohana and my fellow pirate scholars. In their own ways, they offered important contributions to this book—from reading early excerpts to listening to me vent and from offering moral support to sharing my work with the world. And to those across the globe who purchased, read, borrowed, critiqued or gifted my first book: it is your support that not only encouraged me to become vulnerable yet again and publish a second book, but it also no doubt inspired the press to support a second project.

I would be remiss if I didn't extend my sincerest gratitude to the friends, family and loved ones who uplifted, guided and sometimes carried me through this process. To Dr. Emily Contois, who agreed to read an early draft despite the subject being outside of her area of study, your feedback was immensely helpful in driving the use of narrative throughout the text. To my friends and colleagues Drs. Amanda Licastro and Kerry Spencer, there are not words adequate enough to express my gratitude for you. Your unrelenting faith in my abilities and your unwavering support sustained me during periods of depression, self-doubt and loss of confidence. Our late-night wine and Zoom chats give me life. To my parents, Kimberly and Darren; my brothers, Tyler and Kenneth; my grandparents Shirley and Pat; my bonus parents, Steve and Susan; my sisters, Eileen, Kathryn and Joanna; and my forever friends (you know who you are)—I am the person I am today because of the countless ways you have encouraged me, challenged me and loved me. From silly Snapchats to hilarious Instagram reels, from providing a shoulder to cry on to laughing with me at inappropriate times, I am forever grateful for the impact you've had on my life.

Lastly, there can be no acknowledgements page without mention of the tireless love and support of my partner, Kyle, and our babies. Who could have believed that a couple of impetuous kids would make it this far, eleven years and counting? We are not the same people we were at the ripe old age of twenty-three. No, we have quite literally grown up together in these last eleven years. We have faced immense challenges and come out the other side simply because we had each other. There may be a little more gray in your beard, and there might be a few more aches and pains in my back, but I am thrilled to see what the future has in store for us. You are both my anchor (keeping me grounded when necessary) and my hot air balloon (lifting me up when the occasion calls for it). You are the best person I've ever known. And a special thanks for being a significant contributing factor in the double addition to our family all those years ago: T.J. and J.T. Without their need to go outside a million times a day, I might never take a break from my computer. I am made better by their slobbery kisses, their comfy cuddles and their need to have my attention 24/7.

Note: This book contains many excerpts from primary sources that contain misspellings. In order to preserve the sources' authenticity, these errors remain.

PART I

FROM UNLIKELY ALLY TO DISRUPTIVE MENACE: PIRACY IN THE GOLDEN AGE

He was bred to the sea.

—*The case of Samuel Burgess*

1

LET THE CHAOS BEGIN

In 1689, a man named Samuel Burgess found himself a foremast man on a ship named the *Blessed William*, commanded by one Captain William Kidd.[1] He was party to the mutiny that took place on the *Blessed William* when the "officers carried away the ship and left the Captaine [Kidd] on shoar," naming William Mason (part owner of the ship) commander. Their plan? To "go upon the account"—that is, to go pirating. The men were thirsty for adventure and hungry for plunder. They first sailed to the "Coast of Crocus," where they took two Spanish ships before making their way to New York.[2] They landed in New York in 1690 and Commander Mason immediately obtained a commission to attack French vessels from the governor Jacob Leisler. The legality of their commission was debatable, but they used that commission to seize no fewer than six French vessels in a matter of weeks. The ships were brought into the port of New York to be condemned as a lawful prize.[3] One of the ships, *Jacob*, proved to be in better shape than the *Blessed William*, so the pirates (who considered themselves privateers, given their commission) traded ships and continued back to sea to "cruise upon the enemies." While at sea, their destination was put to a vote, according to the ship's code, a set of rules that the pirates were bound to abide by. These rules varied from ship to ship, and not all crews developed a code. But in the case of Commander Mason and his men, they had equal votes on all matters and used those votes to determine their route: to round the Cape of Good Hope or to sail westward.

It was not as simple as it seemed. The men were divided between crew members and those deemed "officers," leading to explosive tension. After a difficult and contentious vote, the results were thus: the men chose to sail westward, while the officers opted to round the Cape of Good Hope. When the men tried to steer the vessel to the west, the officers "refused to take charge of the ship, so that we were forced to submitt to them, and our course was directed round the cape and so to Madagascar, where wee arrived in August 1691."[4] It is here that Burgess claimed he left the pirates to their own designs, choosing instead to remain in Madagascar, a well-known pirate haven, until he could find passage to "some English port." Burgess found himself waiting and waiting until, in 1692, he was "destitute of cloaths and the very necessaries of life."[5] So, when the *Jacob* returned to Madagascar in June, he reentered the employ of the ship, sailing to the "Gulph of Mocca," where the pirates took two ships and, after another brief stay in Madagascar, sailed for New York.[6] They arrived in New York in April 1693, at which time, New York was under the leadership of Colonel Benjamin Fletcher. Fletcher became a well-known friend of the pirates, so when Burgess appealed to Fletcher for protection from piracy prosecution, Fletcher was more than happy to oblige. Fletcher was, after all, empathetic to the pirates' plight. It probably didn't hurt that those same pirates lined Fletcher's pockets with great riches. But Fletcher's protection did not put an end to Burgess's piratical depredations, despite his protestations of innocence.

As this episode suggests, piracy was an important component of the mid-Atlantic economy, especially in New York. Sure, the ships sailing to New York from Boston or the West Indies or from New York or Philadelphia to the West Indies or London were susceptible to attack by pirates—as was the case for a pink laden with wine from Madeira sailing from Boston to New York, which was seized by the pirates on board Black Sam Bellamy's ship, the *Whydah*.[7] There was also an incident in which pirates aboard the *Duke and Duchess* plundered a sloop from New York, which was robbed of almost all its water and provisions, and at least two men were impressed into service.[8] And there was the case of the New York snow the *Eagle*, whose commander was threatened with a cutlass for not bringing to at first shot, and the pirates "threatned [sic] to sink his vessell and throw him overboard with a double-headed shot about his neck, if he concealed where his money was."[9] In light of these incidents, one might wonder "what have the pirates ever done for us?" But on the whole, piracy appeared to bring more money into the colony—or at least to its merchants and governor(s)—than it cost the colony. And pirates preferred to frequent the urban environments of

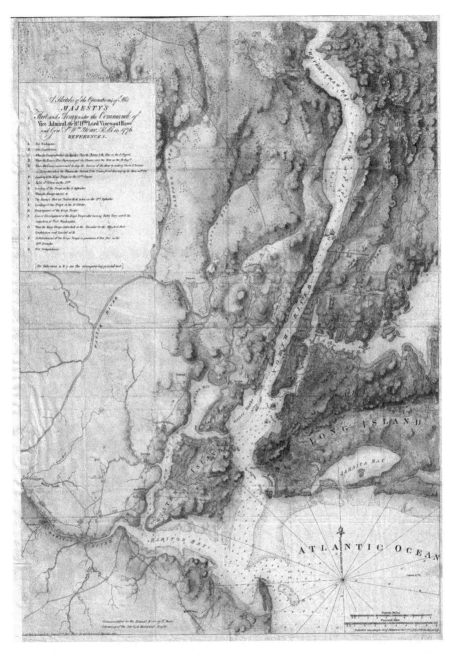

A Sketch of the Operations of His Majesty's Fleet, map by Des Barres of New York Harbor, 1777. *Image from Wikimedia Commons.*

New York City and Philadelphia, where they had their pick of taverns, inns and brothels. For example, Blackbeard was allegedly a patron of the Blue Anchor Tavern in Philadelphia, and it was not uncommon to see men like Blackbeard and Captain Kidd "openly swagger along Water Street and vicinity."[10] Urban environments also made it easier for the pirates to fence their loot, find transient sailors to join their crews and secure the materials to refit and re-provision their ships. And it was the "vast riches of the Red Sea and Madagascar [which] are such a lure to seamen that there's almost no withholding them from turning pirates."[11] So much wealth was to be had that rumors of buried treasure along Philadelphia's waterfront persist to this day.

But what exactly is a pirate, and how does piracy differ from privateering? *Piracy*, at its simplest, is defined as attacking and robbing ships at sea. Before 1700, the terms *buccaneer, freebooter, sea rover* and even *privateer* were used interchangeably with the term *pirate*. One might become a pirate through mutiny on board a merchant vessel or Royal Navy ship. Sometimes, pirate vessels were purchased, and crews, like Stede Bonnet's, were hired. But quite frequently, merchants invested in pirating ventures and colluded with local officials to provide protection to the pirates, who would enrich the port with their spoils. Privateers, however, were legally commissioned commerce raiders, private men of war who were granted letters of marque, or commissions, to attack enemy shipping during times of war. Merchants were responsible for underwriting, or investing in, the privateering venture. The investors were guaranteed between one-third and one-half of the prizes seized. Another share would go to the government for supporting the venture with the letter of marque. The captain and crew of the ship would receive the remainder to split. Essentially, privateers were, like pirates, on a "prey for pay" system, in which they didn't get paid unless they seized a prize. The merchants gambled their ships, while the privateers wagered their lives. Theoretically, letters of marque were only granted during times of war, but in the chaos of the seventeenth and eighteenth centuries, they were often granted by local colonial officials, who were poorly paid, indiscriminately in return for a share of the loot.[12]

When the *Blessed William* arrived in New York, it arrived to a colony in turmoil. After the colony came under the rule of James II of England in 1664, which ended the administration of Peter Stuyvesant and the Dutch West India Company, the king installed a governor who was allowed to choose his own council. Between 1664 and 1685, New York City merchants dominated the "court party," forcing the governors to rely on the backing of these merchants to support an expensive garrison.[13] Then, after 1685, New York had to deal with the aggression of the French on its northern frontier while simultaneously being forced into the Dominion of New England, which placed all the New England and mid-Atlantic colonies together under the rule of a single administrative unit in Boston. Under this dominion, the colonists dealt with the "rapacious" regime of Governor Thomas Dongan, who replaced Sir Edmund Andros.[14] Additionally, they were surrounded by free ports. As such, "before the war, New York was the mart to Pennsylvania, the Jersies and Connecticut, but of late the trade of Pennsylvania has been very near equal to that of New York, and the rest trade for themselves and want little from New York." Additionally, the war with France and ships captured by the French also decreased the revenue, and "dislocating business caused many inhabitants to leave New York, through fear of being detached to defend the frontiers at Albany."[15] So, when, in 1689, the colonists learned that James II had fled to France and that William of Orange and his wife, Mary, were installed as the new king and queen, the colonists immediately— and with great pleasure—overthrew the dominion government. A leading merchant and captain of the militia, Jacob Leisler, became the new leader of the colony, although his leadership was fiercely contested. This was particularly true of those in Albany and Long Island, who outright refused to accept him. The major merchants of the "court party" disbanded, with some going to jail, some going into exile and others fleeing to the country. However, they made their feelings about Leisler known to the English Crown in a letter-writing campaign, placing Leisler in a delicate position.

It was during the insurrection in 1690 that the men of the *Blessed William* arrived in New York. While in port, they easily sold their cargo, which included enslaved Africans, and used their profits to resupply and refit their ship. After the men seized the six French ships and returned to New York in 1691 to have their prizes condemned in Leisler's Admiralty Court (where they would then be sold to supporters of the insurrection), they found themselves in quite a predicament. Leisler was technically no longer in charge, as the letter writing campaign of the "old court" party proved successful. William and Mary sided with the "old court" party, appointing Colonel Henry Sloughter as governor in September 1689.[16] But Sloughter didn't actually make it to New York until March 1691, while his troops had landed in January, which made for an incredibly intense situation. The leader of Sloughter's troops was a man by the name of Colonel Richard Ingoldsby, who demanded that Leisler surrender, while Ingoldsby awaited the arrival and instructions of Sloughter.

A Portrait of King James II, circa the seventeenth century. *Courtesy of the New York Public Library.*

Of course, Leisler, ever the politician, said no and holed away in Fort James along with a number of his adherents. But because of Sloughter's delay, Ingoldsby did not attack the fort until the tension overflowed into an exchange of gunfire on March 17, leaving many dead and wounded. When Sloughter finally arrived, he found a city in chaos. William Kidd, who had been mutinied against by the men of the *Blessed William*, decided that his best chances for advancement—and revenge—lay with the new government. So, he offered himself and his ship, the *Antigua*, in service to Ingoldsby, who dispatched Kidd to Sloughter's ship to notify him of the situation. Sloughter and his troops were able to seize Leisler and his men from the fort, where they were brought to trial for their alleged crimes, including treason and murder. The event was actually "an orgy of revenge," according to historian Robert C. Ritchie, in which the "court party" was not satisfied until Leisler and his second-in-command, Jacob Milborne, were not only hanged but also beheaded. Anti-Leislerians also demanded that Leisler's adherents be jailed or banished into exile.[17]

In the meantime, Kidd quickly began schmoozing his way into Sloughter's good graces. Sloughter's first act as governor was to convene his own admiralty court to discern the activities of Leisler's so-called privateers. Kidd brought suit against the *Pierre*, one of the French ships that the men of the *Blessed William* had captured under their commission from Leisler. Kidd argued that Leisler had no authority to convene an admiralty court, and therefore, the vessel hadn't yet been properly condemned as a prize and, as such, couldn't yet be sold. Kidd smugly won his case. Sloughter condemned the ship as a prize and sold it to prominent merchant Frederick Philipse, who we will see was a huge supporter of piracy in the mid-Atlantic. Philipse purchased the vessel for $500, and Sloughter gave part of the profit of the sale to Kidd, who then financially gained from the piracy of his former crew.[18]

But not all was well in the new government. Sloughter inherited a colony with weak defenses and an even weaker economy. And he died shortly after his arrival in the summer of 1691. He was temporarily succeeded by Ingoldsby before being replaced by Colonel Benjamin Fletcher. Fletcher's main task was to prevent the French from invading the colony of New York. Fletcher was chosen to lead New York due to his extensive experience as a professional soldier who distinguished himself during King William's campaigns in Ireland. He not only governed New York, but he also simultaneously directed the war against the French and Native peoples in the region and, for a two-year period, governed Pennsylvania while taking command of the militias from Connecticut, Rhode Island and New Jersey.[19]

This was no easy task, and Fletcher relied heavily on the wealthy merchant community of New York for support.

As governor, Fletcher sided with the anti-Leislerian party and made allies among the New York merchant community. He even retained the members of Sloughter's executive council, which included the prominent merchants Nicholas Baird, Stephen van Cortlandt, William Nicoll and Frederick Philipse. He curried their favor by granting them large tracts of very valuable land, and he granted them new manors with semifeudal rights.[20] Philipse, who, by 1693, was the richest man in the province, consolidated all of his land holdings into a ninety-thousand-acre estate he named Philipse Manor, and in 1697, van Cortlandt followed suit by consolidating his land holdings into Cortlandt Manor.[21] Fletcher was easily bribed, accepting money, jewels and even ships to ignore the illicit activities occurring within the colony. When Edward Coates and the *Jacob* returned, the pirates reportedly brought in £16,000 (including 2,800 pieces of eight), each man having earned a share of at least £800. The men paid £100 each for protection against piracy prosecution, and as a token of their appreciation for the governor's hospitality, they gave him their ship, which he sold for approximately £800.[22] Furthermore, the crew, as a whole, allegedly gave Fletcher £700 to permit the *Jacob* to come trade.[23] And when Captain Hore (or Hoar) returned to New York after his piratical adventures, Lord Bellomont discovered that "two and twenty of the principal merchants of the town and several members with the secretary and the clerk of the council were interested in the cargo." Pirates would later depose how they bargained with Fletcher for pardons or the sale of their ships and ladings to council members at reasonable rates.[24] Piracy was turning out to be good business for the merchants of the mid-Atlantic.

Yet the economy of the mid-Atlantic also suffered from the attacks of French privateers against their Atlantic shipments, on which they were wholly dependent. Since ships were often unable to sail to and from New York and Philadelphia without fear of attack, the only way the local economy could witness growth was through piracy of the inhabitants' own making.

First, merchants and local businesses, like taverns, inns and brothels, benefited from pirates' arrival to the mid-Atlantic colonies. The pirates would refit and reprovision their ships while enjoying some land-based entertainment before their next voyage. The pirates "swaggered through the streets with purses full of hard money—Arabian dinars, Hindustani mohurs, Greek byzants, French louis d'or, [and] Spanish doubloons."[25] Merchants not only sold pirates the supplies they needed, but they also fenced their loot for them. They didn't care whether their cargo were

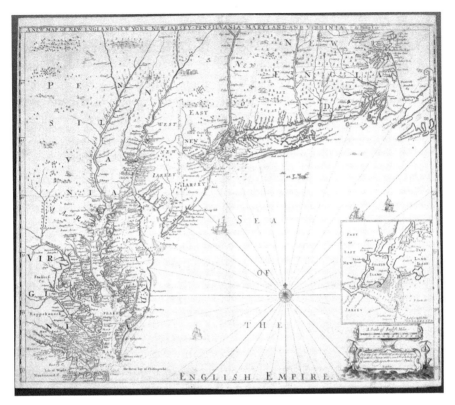

A map of the mid-Atlantic by Phillip Lea, 1690. *Courtesy of the New York Public Library.*

enslaved Africans or sugar, logwood or ambergris, as long as it was a valuable commodity, it was fair game, including "tobacco, wool, tea, rum, brandy, wine, rice, molasses," et cetera.[26] Merchants could reap massive profits—as great as "200, 300, yea sometimes 400" percent.[27] The ports of the mid-Atlantic abounded with illegal traders and illicit goods, as one representative observed that the province of New York was "a noted receptacle of pirates and seat of illegal trade."[28] And pirates usually sold these items to merchants for cheaper prices, as they had little to no overhead.[29] This was especially true after the passage of the 1696 Navigation Acts. William Penn, for example, felt that the acts and the efforts to eradicate piracy and illicit trade were just "thinly veiled attempts" at permitting the taking of a man's property without due process.[30]

The acts essentially required that all goods or merchandise be imported, exported or carried between English possessions in Africa, Asia and America or shipped to England or Wales in English-built or colony-built ships that had to be wholly owned by the English. The masters and three-fourths of the mariners of the ships had to be English citizens. In order to enforce the acts, the acts required the registration of all ships and owners. This included taking an oath that they would have no foreign owners before the ship would be considered English-built. Exceptions included foreign-built ships taken as prizes or those the navy employed for importing naval stores from the colonies. In the past, most of the customs collection and enforcement in the colonies was performed by the governor or his appointees, but evasion, corruption and indifference was common. The acts ultimately tightened English control over the colonies. Exchange in colonial maritime communities like New York and Philadelphia took place as often on water as it did on land. Penn warned colonial administrators that merchants in the colonies would be concerned about having their interests overruled by the admiralty office and feared that the admiralty office would take their ships away from them without the benefit of a jury.[31] Prior to the 1696 acts, piracy trials were conducted under a statute of 1536, which had no provision for piracy trials to occur in the colonies. This meant that pirates captured in the colonies had to be sent to London for trial at the expense of the colony. Jamaica tried to remedy this by passing an act in 1681, which enabled piracy trials to take place on the island, and other colonies were encouraged to adopt their own version of the Jamaica Act. But a jurisdictional flaw meant that the North American colonial courts were unable to try admiralty cases. This was remedied by the 1696 acts, which required colonies to establish their own vice admiralty courts to hear prize cases of privateers and to settle maritime disputes. This was further solidified by a 1700 piracy law that enabled vice admiralty courts to try piracy cases directly.[32]

Second, New York merchants supplied pirates in Madagascar, an island they knew well because of their engagement in the trade of enslaved Malagasy people. New York merchants were able to avoid direct competition with the Royal African Company's monopoly in West Africa, which meant that the merchants were able to purchase enslaved Africans at a barbaric fraction of the price. While they were stealing enslaved Africans, they could, in turn, supply pirates with everything from liquor to guns, gunpowder to clothing. And in return, pirates would supply them with "expensive textiles, drugs, spices, jewels, gold, and currency."[33] In 1693, the *Charles* arrived in St. Mary's from New York, sent by Frederick Philipse, with "severall sorts of goods." The ship contained two cargoes, one for the captain to "dispose of" and one for Adam Baldridge, containing some clothes, shoes, hats, "5 barrells of rum, four Quarter caskes of Madera wine, ten cases of spirits" and some cannon powder. In return, Baldridge sent back "1,100 pieces of 8/8 and dollars, 34 slaves, 15 head of cattel, [and] 57 barrs of iron."[34] Baldridge then sold some of the items he had procured from Philipse to the pirate Captain Thomas Tew, who arrived in St. Mary's, having taken a ship that belonged to the Moors. Each man had a £1,200 share.

Some pirates, like Black Sam Bellamy, took advantage of this trade. In May 1717, Andrew Turbett and Robert Gilmor informed Governor Alexander Spotswood of Virginia that the *Agnis* was taken and sunk by the pirate Samuel Bellamy five leagues off the coast of Cape Charles, Virginia, on April 7. On the same day, Bellamy took the *Ann*, a galley of Glasgow; the *Endeavor*, a pink of Brighthelmstone; and, on April 12, a ship belonging to Leith, all bound for Virginia. Most of the pirates were natives of Great Britain and Ireland, along with twenty-five Black men who had been seized from a Guinea ship. Bellamy and his men declared that they intended to cruise for ten days off Delaware Bay and ten days more off Long Island "in order to intercept some vessels from Philadelphia and New York, bound with provisions to the West Indies."[35] Another pirate, Captain Jacobs, brought a number of goods to St. Mary's, the account of which was drawn up by Frederick Philipse. He sold rum for between three and five pieces of eight per gallon, wine for three pieces of eight per gallon or one piece of eight per bottle, one barrel of beer for sixty pieces of eight, a tanker of beer for one piece of eight, lime juice for four pieces of eight a gallon, sugar for four

The bell from the pirate ship *Whydah*, circa the eighteenth century. *Image from Wikimedia Commons.*

reales a pound and other items, like tar, salt, peas, paper, hats, shoes and tobacco pipes.[36]

The pirate haven at St. Mary's, off the coast of Madagascar, was the design of Adam Baldridge, whom Frederick Philipse of New York had sent to the island. He arrived on the island in 1691 and quickly established a fortified trading post next to one of the most defensible harbors in the world. Baldridge essentially provided pirates of the Red Sea a base that they could return to between ventures, which meant they no longer had to return immediately to the colonies in the west to resupply and refit.

Baldridge recounted that in 1692, the *Nassau* arrived under the command of Edward Coates. The *Nassau* careened at St. Mary's, during which time, Baldridge supplied it with "cattel for their present spending…and for the cattel I had two Chists [chests] and one jarr of powder, six great guns and a quantity of great shott, some spicks and nails, five bolts of duck [canvas] and some twine, [and] a hogshead of flower." After their trade, the *Nassau* set sail to return to New York, with each man having earned approximately £500.[37]

Robert Quarry informed the commissioners of customs that the "Madagascar trade is the only voyage now thought of in these parts" and that the merchants of New York were able to build their estates because of it. He observed that they ventured to the Madeiras, where "they take a loading of wine and brandy, and from thence directly to Madagascar, where they meet the pirates and purchase their plunder on very easy term[s]." Then they returned to New York, where they had "all the security in the world to land their goods."[38] According to Lord Bellomont, the governor of Massachusetts, there was "frequent trade between this [New York] and Madagascar; the pirates, who fitted out in this port [New York], bringing their spoils taken in the East Indies and the Red Sea to that island, whence merchant ships from this port, publicly loaded with goods useful to the pirates, brought them back here for sale."[39] A practice was set up so that the spoils taken by the pirates (set out from New York) would be brought to the city in merchant ships, whose owners were also interested in the pirates' ships. Bellomont further referred to the city of New York as a "nest of pirates" and observed that Fletcher had "embezzled and converted to his own use large sums of money."[40] While the city seemed to be losing money, Fletcher and his cronies were becoming wildly wealthy through illegal trade.[41]

Bellomont provided the *Fortune* as an example, "commissioned by Colonel Fletcher as a privateer but publicly loaded here, went to Madagascar and brought back East India goods from the ship of the pirate Hore [Hoar], who had also a commission from Colonel Fletcher."[42] In his deposition, John Pantree admitted to serving on board the *Fortune*, which sailed to Madagascar and took in "a cargo of sugar, liquors, pumps, hats and stockings, arms and gunpowder at Turtle Bay." While in Madagascar, the crew traded for enslaved Africans and also traded with a vessel "formerly commanded by one Hore [Hoar] (who was then dead) for East India goods." The men brought the said goods to Long Island Sound, where they were "taken off by two New York sloops."[43] Pantree's deposition was supported and confirmed by the deposition of Edward Taylor, who recalled "receiving pirates' goods at Madagascar."[44]

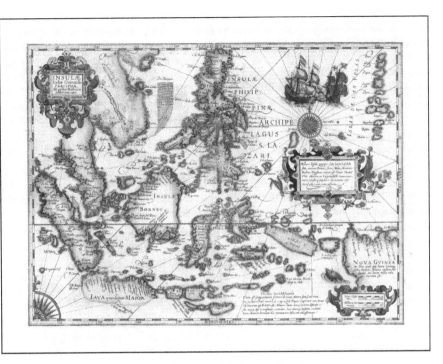

A map of the East Indies by Jodocus Hondius, 1606. *Image from Wikipedia.*

Taylor further deposed that a "bargain [was] made by him, on behalf of the [pirate] ship's crew, with Colonel Fletcher and Mr. William Nicoll of the council" for the "rewards that they were to have and did receive from the said Taylor and his company."[45] Taylor promised Fletcher and Nicoll "£700…if the ships might be brought in and protections given to the crew….The promise of £700 could not be fulfilled because the crew had dispersed, so the owners made the governor a present of the ship. The crew also collected £200 afterwards as a present to Nicoll."[46] According to Bellomont, he seized the *Fortune* and its goods, condemning it. The ship itself was only valued at £297. The merchants were "so much incensed" by his actions and had "so far corrupted the evidence that it was hard to procure enough to condemn the ship and goods." Additionally, they terrified the witnesses and "daily curse and threaten the few persons that have assisted me in the king's service."[47] The merchants had "grown rich together with him [Fletcher] by fitting out pirate ships and trading with Madagascar, Scotland and Curaçao." The merchants, "being instruments of his maladministration," justified Fletcher's actions and thanked him for his service to trade.[48]

Bellomont also remarked on Robert Glover, a pirate who allegedly had a commission from Fletcher. Glover's ship lay within sight of the fort there for several days, and Bellomont was told that trade occurred between Glover and Fletcher. Glover's design of going to the Red Sea being very public, it was likely that Fletcher was so cautious as to give him a commission privately and not let it be registered. As evidence, the deposition of Henry Watson, who was taken prisoner by the pirates in 1696, illustrated Fletcher's complicity. He recounted how the pirates stated that "they had a commission from the governor of New York to take the French." According to Watson, both Fletcher and the governor of Rhode Island "knew their designs." The pirates, he said, were Hoar and Glover.[49] Further, the information from Watson revealed that he could "prove that Governor Fletcher received £400 for a commission from the pirate Robert Glover, provided that he were secured from future trouble at Governor Fletcher's hands."[50] Shortly thereafter, four more ships came to Bellomont to be cleared, but he delayed them, believing them "to be bound to Madagascar to supply the pirates with necessaries and to bring back their goods, and that I believed that each ship ought to give security not to trade with pirates."[51]

One of those whom Bellomont delayed was pirate trader Giles Shelley, whose "cargo outwards was of very small value, but the returns mentioned in his letter are exceedingly great and prove the nature of his trade." Mr. Stephen Delancey, to whom Shelley wrote, was one of the merchants involved with Captain Thomas Moston's *Fortune*.[52] Another was Captain Burgess. Many in the council, however, were invested in these ships and "unanimously opposed this method" so that Bellomont was forced to allow the ships to proceed on their voyages.[53] Meanwhile, the Council of Trade and Plantations gave Bellomont full authority to "continue to use his utmost endeavours to seize all goods imported contrary to the Acts of Trade [1696], as likewise all persons that may be justly suspected of piracy, either as principals or abettors, and to punish them with the utmost severity of law."[54] They also stripped some authority away from the governors of Pennsylvania and West Jersey, because there seemed to be "little ground of depending upon the safe custody of the pirates seized in Pennsylvania" nor any expectation that a proper punishment would be inflicted on them. And because there was no "act in force in West New Jersey by which those seized in that Province can be tried and punished there," the council "humbly offer that all pirates seized in Pennsylvania and West New Jersey be sent hither [to England], together with the evidences upon which they

The Buccaneer was a Picturesque Fellow, by Howard Pyle, 1905. *Image from Wikimedia Commons.*

have been seized and which may be of any use for their conviction here, that so they may be tried and punished according to law."[55]

Bellomont further complained to the Council of Trade and Plantations that Frederick Philipse was but one merchant who was getting filthy rich from his connections with Madagascar. Philipse's ship "and the other two come from Madagascar, which are expected every day" in New York, would "abound with gold." According to Bellomont, "'tis the most beneficial trade, that to Madagascar with the pirates, that ever was heard of, and I believe there's more got that way than by turning pirates and robbing." He heard that the pirate trader, Giles Shelley of New York, sold "rum, which cost but 2s. per gallon" at New York for a whopping "50s. and £3 per gallon at Madagascar." Shelley also sold a pipe of Madeira wine, which cost him £19 in New York, which netted him £300 from Madagascar. It was "strong liquors and gunpowder and ball [that] are the commodities that go off there to best advantage," and four ships from the previous summer "carried thither great quantities of those things."[56]

Additionally, Bellomont wrote that since New York, one of the four ships had come in that went from New York to Madagascar last summer. The

Brooklyn: Bird's Eye View of the City of New York, by John Bachmann, 1859. *Courtesy of the New York Public Library.*

ship brought sixty pirates and a vast deal of treasure. Bellomont heard that every one of the pirates had paid £50 for his passage, and the owners of the ship cleared £30,000 through this voyage. The chief owners of the ship were Shelley, Mr. Hackshaw and Stephen Delancey, a "hotheaded, sawey Frenchman and Mr. Hackshaw's correspondent." Shelley allegedly earned £8,000 from that voyage for his own share, and he made some purchases in New York upon his return from Madagascar.[57] Bellomont also learned that there were two hundred pirates in Madagascar who intended to take their passage in Frederick Philipse's ship and two others belonging to New York. Further, a "great ship has been seen off this coast," which was said to have been commanded by one Maise, a pirate "who has brought a vast deal of wealth from the Red Seas."[58]

The merchants of New York fought back, accusing Bellomont of being an adherent to the traitorous Leisler. They stated that he had taken the bones of Leisler and laid them "publicly in state for about three weeks and, afterwards, reburied in the Dutch Church, against the consent of those who had the custody and care of it, with great pomp and solemnity." They contended that Bellomont had "displaced most of the council, sheriffs and justices of the peace and put in their places mean, ignorant people, mostly of Leisler's party" and "arbitrarily and illegally imprisoned several persons and threatened to treat others likewise unless they would take a general oath to answer all questions he should propose to them." But their biggest gripe? Bellomont had "stopped several ships after they were cleared, to the great loss of their owners, without reason assigned." In particular, he held the *New York Merchant*, under Commander Thomas Jeffers, for about three weeks.[59] According to a letter from the Council of Trade and Plantations to Lord Bellomont, the merchants were "concerned in the province of New York" that he intended to install a government loyal to the memory of Leisler "to the great hazard of their effects there." Further, the merchants "dare not, they say, send any goods therefore to New York, but like many of the inhabitants, are only anxious to withdraw."[60] The merchants were also "exasperated" with Bellomont because he would not do as Fletcher did. Instead, Bellomont "discouraged" the pirates and prevented eight pirate ships from coming to the town for three months. The merchants claimed that Bellomont had "ruined the town by hindering privateers (as they called pirates)" from bringing in £100,000 since his arrival.[61]

2

FORTUNE AND MISERY
IN THE MID-ATLANTIC

New York wasn't the only port to play host to unsavory characters. Colonel Quarry, judge of the admiralty court in Pennsylvania, complained to the Council of Trade and Plantations that there was not so much as a proclamation against the pirates. Several known pirates were allowed to live and trade in Pennsylvania, trading primarily with Curaçao, to the "great damage of honest traders."[62] He apprehended eight alleged pirates, "in spite of the inhabitants' endeavours to prevent" him. Of the pirates committed to prison, most were out on bail very quickly. According to Quarry, "They walk the streets with their pockets full of gold and are the constant companions of the chief in the government." They threatened Quarry's life as well as the lives of those who were active in apprehending them. The pirates carried their prohibited goods publicly in boats from one place to another to market, threatened the lives of the king's collectors and, "with force and arms, rescued their goods from them." The favor that the pirates curried in Pennsylvania and the Jerseys "hath been of a very fatal consequence to several of H[is] M[ajesty's] subjects, who have had their ships and goods carried out of this port by their own ships' crews." And those who "never designed to do an ill thing, seeing pirates and murderers at liberty," making certain persons great sums of money, it "encourages them to turn villains, too." According to Quarry, the 2,000 pieces of eight he had taken from two of the pirates declared their intention to "bring their action against me for it, being encouraged thereto by this government." And Quarry was sure that with the local government's aid, the pirates would recover their money.[63] Governor Markham of Pennsylvania, he said, was "pleased to give pirates their liberty when committed for piracy." He would pay them a visit in his coach when they were in jail, and when they had paid their compliments to him, they were let out.[64] Governor of Virginia Francis Nicholson supported Quarry's complaints, arguing in July 1698 that "several of them [the pirates] are in Pennsylvania, where the government, owing to the Quakers falling out among themselves, is very loose." Nicholson also questioned whether the Quaker-led government would be able to defend itself militarily and whether it could even imprison pirates if the Crown ordered the colony to do so.[65]

Quarry also suggested that Pennsylvanians couldn't get by without illicit trade. In September 1698, an express was sent to Quarry from Philadelphia. The note stated that all the seized goods in the custody of the marshal had been forcibly carried away by warrant of Anthony Morris, a justice of the peace. Quarry first thought that Morris had acted out of ignorance, but when Governor Markham refused Quarry's demand that the goods be restored, he found that "it was the act of the whole government; so now they have thrown off the vizard and openly affront the king's authority." When Pennsylvanians found that all their threats could not frighten Quarry from his duty—at least according to him—and that their "beloved, profitable, darling, illegal trade, must be ruined, they resorted, having no other game to play, to open disobedience and contempt." He argued that they "have so long encouraged illegal trade by exporting tobacco to Scotland and importing European goods from Curaçao, gaining great advantage thereby, that they will not part with it." Moreover, Quarry decried that unless the illegal trade be checked, the people will "cease to depend on England for supplies but, by the plenty and cheapness of the commodities, will be able to supply the other colonies and to ruin trade."[66]

But the Pennsylvania General Assembly wrote to King William of Orange that, as for pirates, they knew of none that had been entertained there except Robert Clinton, Edmund Lassells, Peter Clausen and "some others supposed to be of Every's crew." The pirates who happened to travel there, as they did in some of the neighboring colonies, were apprehended on suspicion of being pirates and bound over to the sessions. But as soon as the lords justices' order against pirates was received, they were confined in Philadelphia County Jail. It was from here that they made their escape to New York, where they were at first arrested and then released without trial.[67] According to the general assembly, no one in Pennsylvania had "advanced their fortunes by piracy or illegal trade." And as for those who "came here

An Attack on a Galleon (an illustration of pirates approaching a ship), by Howard Pyle, 1905. *Image from Wikimedia Commons.*

as travellers about seven years ago and were supposed to be pirates," they settled and "claimed the liberties of English subjects among us," encouraged by Edward Randolph, who "gave expectation of pardon to some of them." This, along with the assistance they received from Colonel Fletcher, "gave them further encouragement to continue among us, though we can sincerely say that their settling here was a great grief to many." But according to the assembly, "Some of them are gone, others are dead, and the rest shall be arrested as soon as facts appear to require such procedure or the king shall order it."[68]

Yet Robert Snead told the story a little differently. He claimed that he felt it was his duty as a "subject and a magistrate" to apprehend Henry Every, whose alias was Bridgman, and the rest of the rogues who ran away with the ship *Fancy*, committing several piracies in the Rattan Seas. Snead said that he went at once to the governor and told him that several of Every's men were in Pennsylvania. Governor Markham said he had not heard that. Instead, Markham said, "If people came here and brought money, he was not obliged to ask them whence they came." No sooner was Snead gone than Markham sent and "acquainted the pirates with what had passed" between them.[69]

According to Snead, it was well known that Markham "had a great present made to him and his family by them and others of the same crew." Snead again thought it his duty to apprehend them and called on two of his fellow justices to join him. But they, knowing the governor's inclinations, at first refused. When Snead threatened to send them to England if they did not join him, however, they finally consented. Three of the pirates were brought before the justices, and there was sufficient proof that they belonged to the *Fancy*. So, Snead ordered them to be sent to jail. But one of his fellows went to the governor, and he and the others bailed the pirates out. Some weeks later, Snead heard from England that the factories were seized and likely to be damaged by the pirates. Snead then seized the pirates again. Markham was "much displeased" with Snead and called him before his council, where he asked what he had against those pirates to hinder their discharge. Snead told him there was proof enough that they were Every's men. The governor once again dismissed the pirates. Snead then issued a warrant to apprehend the old pirates, who he was told had brought £1,000 to Pennsylvania for each man and gave £100 each to Markham.[70] Further, Snead suggested that as long as the government was in the hands of Quakers, as it was at that time, it "must be expected that pirates and unlawful traders will still be encouraged."[71]

Dutch East Indiaman, by Wenceslaus Hollar, 1647. *Courtesy of the Metropolitan Museum of Art.*

And the residents of Newcastle, Delaware, appealed to Governor Markham for aid. Jacob Bodill, a ship's carpenter; James Hunt; and Harman Peterson of Newcastle deposed in July 1699 that Matthew Birch, the collector of Newcastle, was ineffectual in seizing the pirates.[72] Matthew Birch responded that he had "gone as far as I can to prosecute John Minis, James Macomb and Edward Robinson for aiding pirates and running their goods…but no measures I can take prove effectual amongst non-jurors, Quakers and ill-affected Scotchmen."[73] From Boston to Newcastle, "the people have been many of them pirates themselves and to be sure are well affected to the trade. They are so lawless and desperate that I can get no honest man to venture to collect the excise among them and watch their trade."[74] At the end of August 1698, a company of pirates sailed in on "two dark ships flying the black flag" and plundered the town of Lewes, threatening Newcastle. The pirates held eleven of the town's leaders hostage while they ransacked Lewes. The residents claimed that they had no fort, arms or militia and were therefore at the mercy of such "merciless wretches." According to the minutes of the council, dated August 9, 1699, in Philadelphia, the council rejected the residents' petition without explanation.[75] Some believed that the petition was rejected because leaders of the colony thought that the people of Lewes were in cahoots with the pirates and that they received "just punishment for its complicity with the cutthroats."[76]

Collusion abounded along the mid-Atlantic coast. Merchants in New York and Philadelphia would sell most of the expensive luxury goods they received to ports like Hamburg, Germany, which were "conveniently removed from the scrutiny of customs agents."[77] For example, Frederick Philipse was accused of sending his ship, the *Frederick*, with "pirates' plunder at sea" to Hamburg.[78] According to several depositions, some pirates brought approximately £1,500 to £1,800, which they used to purchase land or property. Some, like our friend Samuel Burgess, even entered this trade on his own. After Burgess returned to New York in 1693, he bought a house and found himself employed by Frederick Philipse. Philipse sent Burgess back to Madagascar in order to trade with his former pirate colleagues. Due to a lack of strong government oversight, piracy in New York proliferated under Fletcher's administration. The city became a haven for these nefarious rogues and a center for supplying the pirates who were operating in the Indian Ocean. Buccaneers filled the city's streets, taverns and brothels. And they paid in Turkish and Arabic gold and "strange coins of all kinds," which was highly welcomed in New York's depressed economy.[79]

The cemetery of past pirates at Ambodifototra (St. Mary's Island), Madagascar, 2006. Michipanero. *Image from Wikimedia Commons.*

New York became the land of opportunity for would-be ne'er-do-wells. In the deposition of John Wick, he recounted how, in "April 1696, Josiah Rayner landed at the east end of Long Island," where there was treasure of over £1,000 value in his chest. The sheriff seized the chest on grounds of it being a privateer's goods. Rayner asked Wick for advice on how to recover the chest. So, Wick went to James Emott, who took Wick to Governor Fletcher, "who asked the value of the treasure and, on hearing £1,000, said that he wished it were £2,000." Wick then asked for discharge of the chest and protection for Rayner, who had been one of Tew's crew. Wick promised Fletcher a reward for his assistance. Fletcher said that since Rayner had gone out with his permission, he was right to come to him for protection. Fletcher claimed that though he would take no reward for it, he "would not refuse a present if Rayner should give him one." Fletcher then signed the protection and an order for discharge of the chest, at which time, Wick gave him £50, which Fletcher accepted.[80] According to Lord Bellomont, Rayner's treasure was valued at £1,500. Although Rayner and his chest of money were seized by the sheriff, Colonel Fletcher demanded his release upon receiving a "considerable reward." Soon afterward, Rayner purchased land in New York but fled "on the publication of the proclamation against Every's men." Two men, Emott and Weekes, were believed to have been Rayner's brokers.[81]

Fletcher's assistance to Rayner was just one instance in a long list of collaborative ventures with pirates. On November 23, 1696, a pirate "came under English colours into Calicut Road," where several ships were anchored. When approaching the outermost ship, a pirate "fired a gun at her and then, hoisting Danish colours, fired broadsides and volleys of small shot, laid her on board and took her." From that ship, the pirates fired at the other ships and took three of them, including one of the Mughal's hired ships, a Banyan ship and the English East India Company's frigate *Josiah*. Afterward, five other ships "cut their cables and ran ashore." Having taken four of the ships, the pirates demanded £10,000 in ransom; otherwise, they would burn them. As the company did not immediately have the money, the pirates "hoisted bloody colours, fired one of them and soon after set a second ashore, also on fire." Some of the pirates, when they came ashore to demand the ransom, informed the chief and council that they "acknowledged no countrymen, that they had sold their country and were sure to be hanged if taken, and that they would take no quarter, but do all the mischief they could." A Captain Mason was sent on board the pirates' ship from the English factory, and after a brief detention, he was returned to shore. Mason reported that the pirates were going to cruise for Persia and Bussorah ships and that they had been in Mocha, having left there on August 24. They also confirmed that they were the ones who took the *Arab* at Chuttapore. Their commander was a Dutchman, Dirick Clevers of New York.[82] Clevers told Mason that most of the pirates who infested those seas were fitted out at New York, where they "return a share of their unlawful gains, the governor conniving thereat." He also informed Mason that the pirate Gilliam's ship, after their piracies in the Indian seas, returned to New York and shared £700 for each man. They then "made a present of their ship to the governor, who sold her for £1,000; and shortly afterwards, £2,000 was offered to the buyer by some of the crew who intended to pursue their evil practices."[83] Clevers technically had a commission from Governor Fletcher, granted in 1694, for his ship, the *Resolution*. It was a large ship, with twenty guns, and Clevers was known to show no mercy. After plundering the East India ships the *Ruparel* and the *Calicut Merchant*, Clevers burned them with their crew still on board. Clevers was supported by the notorious John Hoar in the *John and Rebecca*. He, too, had a privateering commission from Fletcher.[84]

Captain Thomas Warren of HMS *Windsor* further reported to the English East India Company that the master of a ship from Madagascar gave him an account of a small island called Santa Maria (St. Mary's) in the northeast region of Madagascar, where the pirates have a "very commodious harbour, to which they resort and clean their ships." Here, he said, the pirates had built a fortification of forty or fifty guns. They had about 1,500 men, with seventeen "sail of vessels, sloops and ships, some of which carry forty guns." According to the informant, the pirates were furnished from New York, New England and the West Indies with "stores and other necessaries." Warren was informed, however, that if the pirates were granted pardons, "they would leave that villainous way of living."[85]

It was difficult to ignore the prosperity that pirates like these afforded the mid-Atlantic colonies. Pirates brought so much hard specie, or currency, into the colonies that there were more silversmiths than lawyers, as silversmiths fenced the loot for the pirates. According to historian Mark Hanna, this helps explain the abundance of silversmiths in regions that were technically suffering from a monetary crisis.[86] Approximately half the coins that existed in colonial America were Spanish reales. And the monetary practices of many colonies were designed to encourage piracy. East Jersey and Pennsylvania, for example, raised the value of Spanish coins as much as 25 percent, while West Jersey's trade policies drew privateers from New York into Sandy Hook. Colonel Fletcher even declared that "the pirates enrich the

Dutch Ships on a Harbour, by Willem van de Velde I, circa the seventeenth century. *Courtesy of the Metropolitan Museum of Art.*

charter governments."[87] Royal officials worried about how such monetary manipulation might create a "contract bidding war for sea marauders," which would heighten colonial tensions.[88] Nathaniel Higginson lamented to his superiors, "It is certain that these villains frequently say that they carry their unjust gains to" the colonies, where they are permitted to come and go without control, "spending such coin there, in the usual lavish manner of such persons," that it was obvious that they had obtained said coin illegally.[89]

And there was no shortage of pirates, smugglers and other maritime bandits to trade with. Contemporary estimates of the pirate population between 1690 and 1750, according to historian Marcus Rediker, ranged from 1,000 to 2,000—or more—at any given time. In all, approximately 4,500 to 5,500 men (and women) turned to piracy during the late seventeenth and early eighteenth centuries.[90] These pirates always followed the lucrative trade routes and visited profitable ports like New York City and Philadelphia. If we account for so-called privateers, the figure is even higher. What to call these men and women confounded contemporaries. Samuel Taylor Coleridge, who commented on the roles of Elizabethan sea dogs like Sir Frances Drake, said, "No man is a pirate unless his contemporaries agree to call him so."[91] Attorney general of Pennsylvania Robert Quarry frequently complained about the Quakers, who referred to the pirates as "honest men," while he believed, based on eyewitnesses, evidence and testimony, that these men were obviously pirates. Meanwhile, the governor of Pennsylvania William Markham referred to men like his son-in-law as privateers, arguing that they had documents allowing them to prey on enemy shipping. He neglected to mention that they preyed primarily on Mughal ships and that the Mughal emperor was technically an ally. Even William Penn questioned how to define these men. He remarked that it would take "something more than hanging" to cure the local population of their support of piracy.[92]

Nathaniel Coddington, the official register of the admiralty court in Rhode Island, observed that all the commanders of the mid-Atlantic "went to Madagascar and the seas of India and were employed to commit piracy."[93] Many officials were at odds with the gentry class, who favored local traditions and customs, even if those traditions included ignoring maritime depredation in all its forms.[94] Viewing these men not as pirates or maritime marauders was common among the population of the mid-Atlantic and was "evident throughout the Delaware Bay and not only among a handful of gentry grandees."[95] In Pennsylvania, for example, the Quakers were avid supporters of piracy and privateering. When the council composed an act for punishing pirates and privateers, Quakers refused to pass the bill. According to Hanna, the ever-changing usage of terms to describe these "bandits at sea" reflected the "ambiguity of the many roles they played in the colonial world."[96] He argues that "the fluid conditions on the high seas generated a range of designations—privateers, corsairs, private men-of-war, freebooters, interlopers, buccaneers, and smugglers as much as pirates— sometimes applied loosely and at other times very specifically."[97]

Any pirate wishing to retire from their swashbuckling way of life could buy a return passage to New York or Philadelphia for 100 pieces of eight, plus the cost of his own food and drink.[98] One such pirate was Richard Roper, who, in August 1701, deposed that it had been about five years since he had gone with Captain Kidd, commander of the *Adventure Galley*, from England to New York and from New York to the Red Sea. He recounted taking many Moorish ships before returning to Madagascar, where he left Kidd and joined Captain Culliford aboard the *Resolution*. They, too, seized several Moorish ships. Roper, "being then a boy together with four other boys, had but one man's share" of approximately £700. After they returned to Madagascar, Roper left the *Resolution* and found that Samuel Burgess and the *Margaret* were bound for New York. So he "entered himself a passenger" aboard the *Margaret* with the hopes of returning to the friendly port of New York. But Roper would never make it to New York, as a Captain Lowth seized the men aboard the *Margaret*.[99]

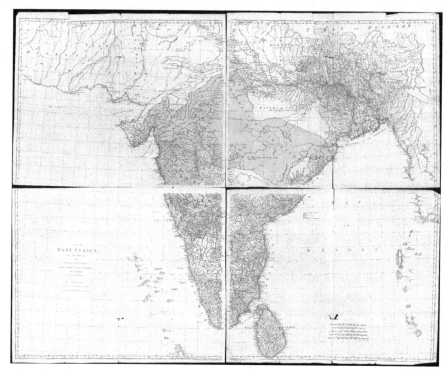

The East Indies with the Roads, map by Thomas Jefferys, 1768. *Image from Wikimedia Commons.*

The mid-Atlantic pirates didn't just affect life in the northern colonies. A colonial merchant named Mr. Gale wrote to Colonel Thomas Pitt Jr. of South Carolina in November 1718 that they needed to "prevent the trade with [the pirates] from Rhoad Island, New York, Pennsylvania, etc., for the pirates themselves have often told me that if they had not been supported by the traders from thence with ammunition and provisions according to their directions, they could never have become so formidable, nor arriv'd to that degree that they have."[100] Philadelphia and New York City were just two cities in a global network that, for two decades, connected colonies to entrepôts, like Madagascar. This trade enabled piracy in the Indian Ocean to thrive.[101] Those pirates who came to Delaware Bay brought with them "colorfully printed calicos and silks in high demand, produced in India, that would, perhaps ironically, adorn Governor Markham's wife and daughter."[102] One visitor observed that pirates arrived "with as much confidence and assurance as the honest men in the world, without any molestation whatever," bringing plunder worth somewhere between £12,000 and £15,000 (roughly $1.5

million to $2 million in today's currency).[103] Governor Fletcher himself made £30,000 in the nearly six years he was in office, which far exceeded his governor's salary. Lord Bellomont remarked that Fletcher had "left no trick or fraud unpractic'd to get money, and all under the mask of a pretended piety."[104] Governor Markham complained that the pirate Thomas Tew "commanded" the "cellar and servants and committed debaucheries in" Fletcher's "house and company," while the two also "exchanged presents, such as gold watches." Although Tew was "a man of infamous character, he was received and caressed by Governor Fletcher, dined and supped with him often and appeared with him publicly in his coach."[105] Tew had allegedly brought in no less than £100,000 to New York and Rhode Island.[106] It was perhaps ironic for Markham to complain about Fletcher's complicity with pirates given his own reputation. It wouldn't be until these communities gained legal and affordable access to luxurious commodities that the communities would increasingly refuse to tolerate piracy.

So, what made the Indian Ocean and Red Sea such desirable locations for pirates to congregate? According to historian James Lydon, it was the rapid decline of the Indian empire of the great Mughal "into decadence and anarchy" that attracted pirates. The English East India Company warred with the Mughal emperor between 1686 and 1689. So, in the

Mouth of the Delaware, by Thomas Birch, 1828. *Image from Wikimedia Commons.*

Entrance to a Dutch Port, by Willem van de Velde II, circa 1665. *Courtesy of the Metropolitan Museum of Art.*

1690s, "gold-seeking pirates flocked like scavengers to feed upon the decaying carcass" of the Mughal's empire. At first, the pirates limited their attacks to Moorish or Indian ships. But the English East India Company viewed the pirates as being bad for business. So, pirates began expanding their piratical depredations to English, French and Dutch vessels. And the pirates made St. Mary's of Madagascar their main haunt. Adam Baldridge had settled in St. Mary's after tricking the Malagasy people and enslaving many of their population. Baldridge was sent to Madagascar to set up a trading depot by none other than our dear friend Frederick Philipse in 1691. Baldridge routinely received shipments of goods from Philipse and other New York merchants. And Philipse was said to clear between £5,000 and £10,000 a venture.[107]

3

THE BATTLE OF THE GOVERNORS

In July 1697, the governor of East and West Jersey Jeremiah Basse wrote a letter to William Popple to say that surely, he could not be "insensible of the dishonour as well as damage suffered by this nation through the increase of piracies under the banner of England in any part of the world." He gave the example of the depredations of Every on the coasts of India and Arabia, which undoubtedly had "come under your cognisance," but he believed that Popple had not been informed of the increase in the number of pirates on the East Coast caused by the "expectation of great riches there and perhaps too much by the connivance of those who ought to have suppressed them." The colonies in the islands and mainland of North America had significantly contributed to this increase. Many of the pirates left some of their wives and families as "pledges of their return behind them." And Basse was advised that four or five vessels were expected to return within a few months with men who belonged to New England, New York and the Jerseys. The pirates would no doubt be emboldened by the good entertainment that they had become used to in those provinces. Basse then asked what was best to be done "with those who have formerly been pirates and are now settled in New Jersey" and "with those that enter the country later, in order to suppress them in time to come." According to Basse, the people "make so much advantage from the currency of their money that they will not be very forward to suppress them, unless it be enjoined on them by a power that they dare not disobey." He informed Popple that he had been taken and "ill-used by some of these men" and thus was filled with a just aversion to them.[108]

But Basse's aggressive antipiracy campaign displeased two powerful factions: the Burlington Quakers in the west and the Perth Amboy Scots in the east. While in Perth Amboy, two gentlemen informed Basse that they had witnessed a couple of men who, because of their "carriage and demeanor," seemed suspicious. So, Basse inquired why Governor Hamilton had not arrested the strangers. Hamilton simply stated that one William Merrick had been arrested but that he had paid his fine and was released. As for the other, he had no knowledge of him. Basse then issued warrants for twenty-three-year-old Merrick and twenty-one-year-old John Elston. After their arrest, they admitted that they were crewmembers of the *Fancy* and that they had participated in the attack on the *Ganj-i-sawai* (anglicized as *Gunsway*) and the blowing up of several mosques. They described how they arrived in East Jersey with several others and quickly "scattered across the colony." One of their crewmates, John Baker, had used his East India loot to pay for a marriage license but had fled after receiving news of Basse's arrival.[109]

Basse had both Merrick and Elston placed in jail, but he was dismayed to find that both men had deep roots in the community. He couldn't even send their treasure back to England because they had converted it into farmland and livestock. Perhaps to placate the locals, Basse promised that the property would remain with the pirates' families. Yet the gentry was so discontent that Basse had to keep additional guards at the jail to prevent the locals from helping the men escape. Furthermore, Basse failed to convince the East Jersey Council to pass an antipiracy bill until March 1699. The council only approved the bill after it had made a number of amendments.

The question of exactly where Merrick and Elston would face trial revealed a long-standing dispute between the Jerseys and New York about which colony had admiralty jurisdiction. Bellomont had ordered that all ships, even those bound to the Jerseys, were required to unload in New York ports and pay fees before heading to the Jerseys. Bellomont feared that if Perth Amboy was a free port, ships would unload there and then smuggle goods into New York. But this rubbed the population of Jersey the wrong way, and the East Jersey Council unanimously voted not to send Merrick and Elston to New York to stand trial. Bellomont then sent a customs official to Perth Amboy Port to seize any ships trading there. But the customs official was accosted by many of the locals, several of whom boarded his ship with clubs, oars and handspikes, threatening to knock his brains out if he seized so much as a single ship. The official, of course, feared for his life and fled back to New York. Despite the East Jersey Council's decision, Basse ultimately made the decision to send the two men to New York, where Bellomont actually released

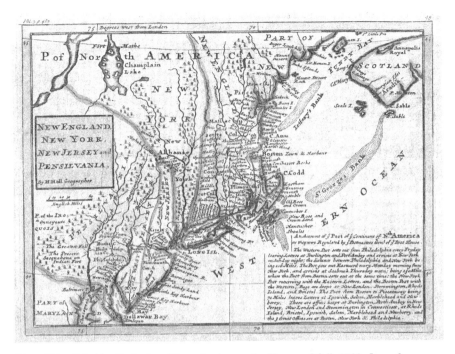

Map of New York, New England, and Pennsylvania, map by Herman Moll, 1729. *Image from Wikimedia Commons.*

them on a relatively small bail. His reasoning? There was insufficient evidence of their guilt. Elston returned to his property and took up life as a farmer, but Merrick allegedly fled New York and returned to a life of piracy. The whole episode proved to the Jerseys that Basse did not have their best interests at heart and that he was a coward who let New York trample all over their rights. So, the locals continued to resist Basse's antipiracy efforts.[110]

William Popple wrote to Basse, approving of his zeal for the suppression of piracy, but he asked for a fuller explanation of certain matters that Basse had hinted at. He asked Basse the following questions:

> *Which are the provinces that have been most blameable in their conduct towards pirates? What particular facts do you know about the pirates or their abettors? Who are the pirates now expected to return and to what particular place? By whom were you yourself taken and ill-used? What methods do you think best for the suppression of pirates, and how do you wish to go about the work? What court is there in New Jersey which can or ever did try pirates, and what law have they there to do it by?[111]*

Basse responded on July 26, 1697, that as far as which of the colonies had been more to blame in their conduct toward pirates, he felt that most of them, "both in the islands and on the main," had been to blame—some through sheer ignorance of their duty, some from their powerlessness to suppress the evil and some, no doubt, from the prospect of gain. According to Basse, those who were most noted for the protection and punishment of pirates when he was in the colonies were Rhode Island, New York, Carolina and Providence. He personally knew "several persons suspected of being concerned in these ill-designs that have been entertained and settled in New Jersey, Pennsylvania, Maryland and Virginia; but those in New Jersey have received a pass from the governor of New York, which obstructs any further enquiry by us." Basse said that he was informed that there was "now out on a piratical voyage the ship *Kent*, formerly commanded by one Ball and now by Thomas Day. She is said to have put in to Carolina, sold all her lading at under rates, taken in men and provisions and gone privateering." He also believed that Popple had undoubtedly heard of Tew and his company, who came into Rhode Island and then to New York before being fitted out again. Tew carried with him the pirate Want in a brigantine and another vessel. They were said to have strengthened themselves by taking a ship belonging to the merchants of New York, commanded by one Glover. They were also reported to have sent remittances to the owners in satisfaction of that depredation. There was another Glover who came from Jamaica, took a rich prize from the French, went afterward to the coast of Guinea and then joined the rest of the pirates on the coast of Arabia. In all, he was told that the pirates were gone from Boston, New York, Pennsylvania, Carolina and Barbados, "from each one ship and from Rhode Island two." There were some others who ran away with a ship that belonged to the local merchants, but they were not yet discovered. The *Nassau* "met one of these rovers at the Cape Bonne Esperance homeward bound from India." Basse was told by the mate of that ship that they were fearful the Dutch would make a prize of the ship. So, they got leave to put some chests of money on board the ship, which were so heavy that six men at the tackles could hardly hoist them in. The chests were given back to the sea rovers, who announced that they were bound for Madagascar.[112]

The persons who were expected to return were Tew's company, all those who sailed from New York and Rhode Island, and it was expected that when they heard of the change of government in New York, they would try to conceal themselves in the Jerseys or Pennsylvania, because the Jerseys had no fort to oppose them. Additionally, the harbor was "little inhabited," so the

*Captain Malyoe Shot
Captain Brand Through
the Head,* by Howard
Pyle, 1896. *Image from
Wikimedia Commons.*

pirates reckoned they would be safe there. Basse said he was told that some people had already been preparing for their reception in the Jerseys. The pirates also entertained a notion that since the Jerseys were not immediately under the king, they couldn't be seized and punished there, which contributed to their boldness.[113]

Basse's zeal for antipiracy came from his own personal experience with pirates. He was taken by a pirate after about six hours' engagement. The ship's commander was a German man, and the ship had thirty guns with 130 men (English, Dutch and French). The fight took place about twenty degrees southeast of Puerto Rico. The pirates took their prisoners to the west end of Hispaniola, where they unloaded one vessel and built their forts on a small island that lay at the bottom of the bay. They then took a sloop, which they sent cruising between Beata Altovalla and Hispaniola, to catch ships bound to the windward side of the island from Jamaica. The pirates used their prisoners "extremely hard, beat us, pinched us of victuals, shut us down in the night to take our lodging in the water cask, detained us 'til they had careened their ship and fitted her for sailing and then, being designed for the coast of Guinea, gave us our liberty."[114]

At the time his letter was written, Basse had already formed schemes for the suppression of piracy and did not doubt that they would be effective if sufficient powers were granted to him. He simply needed the Crown's approval for the government and commission of vice-admiralty within the limits of the Jerseys. Basse knew of no courts in the province with powers sufficient to try pirates, as it was the judgment of the attorney general that they had no admiral jurisdiction. And since piracy should be tried by vice admiralty rather than common law, Basse knew of no one who had been tried for it in the two provinces, and if they had, he feared that they might have demurred to their power. He hoped that this "defect" would be remedied by the king's commissioning of vice-admirals in every mid-Atlantic province.[115] Not everyone was convinced of Basse's motives. Lord Bellomont called Basse the biggest "scoundrel that I ever knew; he will bragg and lye with any man living…and is a rank coward."[116]

Basse joined forces with Quarry in late 1699, scouring the Jersey countryside for pirates. But many of the pirates allegedly escaped to Long Island and Rhode Island because "the generality of the people are too willinge to give assistance and encouragement to these sort of people." Some pirates did choose to surrender to Basse and Quarry, but even then, the Quakers did their best to bail them out. Many of the men who were captured carried immense amounts of money or treasure on their person, although they certainly would have spent much of it in their journeys from port to port. For example, Zion Arnold and John Eldridge were "found in possession of about 7,830 pounds of melted silver, some Arabian gold, silks, and necklaces," while a pirate named William Stanton (who eluded Basse and Quarry) reportedly carried away 2,300 pieces of gold. According to Hanna, the "receipts describing the treasure discovered in the possession of these men suggest the sizable quantities that had already been infused into the local population."[117]

Further, Governor Basse wrote to Popple in April 1698 that things seemed to have calmed. The only event since his arrival took place on April 9: a pirate came into Sandy Hook, landed some men on shore and killed several hogs. Some of the pirates told the people that they belonged to Rhode Island and that, shortly, there would be four or five Red Sea pirates on the coast. Basse informed Lord Bellomont at once, but the pirates, after hearing of the change of governors both in New York and the Jerseys, put out to sea. Basse remarked that he wished that some way might be found to suppress the "sea wolves" and secure the East India trade.[118]

Governors Hamilton and Fletcher were not the only ones caught with their hands in the cookie jar. Governor Markham of Pennsylvania found himself in the hot seat in November 1697 for the "entertainment of Captain Day." Apparently, Captain Day went with his ship and cargo to South Carolina, where he sold both and bought a brigantine under pretense of carrying part of the lading and effects home. So, he had his clearing from the government and gave bond and security to the naval officer for landing his enumerated commodities in England, as the law required. With this clearing, he came to Pennsylvania. But he had more than the ordinary number of men, which made some people "jealous [suspicious] that he designed some other voyage." However, this was "but jealousy." Mr. Jones told Markham that he believed Day had some ill design, because he sold his owner's ship and goods in Carolina. Markham countered that Day had brought his clearing from South Carolina and that there was no information against him. But if there was a complaint, Markham would seize Day. This was provided that Jones gave security to indemnify him, which Jones refused to do. Sometime after this, a French privateer on the coast took several vessels that were coming out of New York, and among them was one of great value that belonged to Philadelphia.[119] The ship was estimated to be worth £9,000.[120]

The French privateer came to the capes of Delaware and cruised there for some time. This put the country into "great consternation not only for fear of their shipping but being apprehensive lest the privateers should land, being distressed for provisions." As concern about the privateer reached great heights, Markham called on Colonel Quarry and told him he was concerned about how to manage this affair. Quarry told him that this could not have happened at a better time, as Captain Day was in town and had a "gang of brisk fellows." He advised Markham to add thirty or forty men from the lower counties to Day's crew and to give Day a commission to command them. By keeping a good lookout, he may ambush the French if they land and cut them off before they could recover their boats. Markham took Quarry's advice, and Day gladly offered his services to go out and fight the French, though they had more than twice his strength, if he could have more men. Day promised to do this without charging the government of Pennsylvania very much money. Thus, Quarry claimed, Markham did nothing wrong and was not guilty of colluding with pirates, despite what others thought.[121]

Yet that didn't stop people from charging the governor with aiding and abetting the pirates. Captain Josiah Daniell wrote to Governor Markham eight months earlier to inform him that three men had run away with the barge belonging to his ship. Daniell supposed they were headed to Pennsylvania because the "worst sailors know how ready you are to entertain and protect all deserters, to the great prejudice of the king's service and to trade (except to your own quaking subjects who never did the king and kingdom any service)." Daniell demanded that "strict enquiry" be made so "that these deserters may be brought to punishment for a terror to others." Further, Daniell argued that it was "ruin for any ships to lade here so long as they have such encouragement to run to your parts, whence they are allowed to" go "trampuseing" (on piratical voyages) where they please. Daniell claimed that he read in the previous July's *Gazette* a proclamation to apprehend Captain Every and his crew but heard that some of Every's men were in Pennsylvania. Some persons had informed Daniell that the deserters from his ship "appeared daily in public and offered their services to several masters in Philadelphia." He wondered if Markham preferred to "gratify them rather than have regard to the king's service."[122]

Markham was having none of that nonsense. He retorted in a letter back to Captain Daniell that his letter was "so indecent that it seems rather penned in the cook room than the great cabin; but I take it as one of your inconsiderate actions and place it to your accustomed conversation." Markham promised that he would, indeed, secure his men if they were found in Pennsylvania. And he said he would do "all things else for the king's service," notwithstanding Daniell's "vilifying of us." Markham replied that it was quite far from his ship's location to Pennsylvania—"no less than the whole length of Maryland." He asked how it was that Daniell's men had passed so quietly through that province "without any notice taken by you," though Daniell jumped to conclusions about Pennsylvania's character and vilified the province's inhabitants. Markham stated that he did not know what Daniell meant by "trampuseing," unless he "aimed at French to show your breeding, which you have ill set forth in your mother tongue." Further, he recounted how he had, for many years, served on men-of-war and that it was their custom, if they thought any men would run away, not to leave the oars and sails in the boat. Instead, they would keep a "good watch and often to hang our boats in the tackles." Markham concluded his letter by saying that he hoped he did not cross paths with Daniell, lest his treatment "be such as I find in your letter." He then wished Daniell a "good voyage and a better temper."[123]

Edward Randolph also accused Markham of colluding with the pirate James Miller, a Scotchman, and some of his company, who, after their arrival to Pennsylvania, paid Markham for his favor and protection.[124] Further, Randolph claimed that five or six vessels came from the Red Sea. Some went south toward Carolina and Providence. But some of them arrived in Pennsylvania, where Governor Markham continued as their steady friend. He entertained some of Every's men, letting two of them go to Carolina, and he allowed the other two to stay in the province, despite having the lords justices' proclamation against them. One of the pirates, Claus, kept a shop in Philadelphia. Another of them, James Brown, married Markham's daughter, and they lived near Newcastle.[125] Markham countered that he had "doubted Mr. Randolph's honesty ever since the first pirates landed at the capes of Delaware Bay," when Randolph wrote to a magistrate there that if the pirates would give him £200, he would procure pardons for them.[126] But Lord Bellomont corroborated Randolph's accusations. There were nine pirates wanted for their robberies on the high seas. Dr. Robert Bradenham, who was Kidd's surgeon, was the "obstinatest and most hardned of 'em all." Bradenham had allegedly left 624 pieces of gold with Parson Edward Portlock, a minister of the Church of England in Pennsylvania, and another 100 pieces of gold with a Philadelphia doctor.[127] Brown, he said, was actually married to Colonel Markham's daughter. According to Brown, Markham had him arrested, but then he promptly paid his £300 bail and a bond for good behavior. Markham was stuck in a difficult position. He was clearly heavily invested in illicit trade, his wife and daughter always wearing East India fineries, yet his hand was forced when it came to pushing through antipiracy legislation.[128] David Evans was tried at the Old Bailey Courthouse in London and acquitted. Terlagh Sulivan claimed he was "forced on board a pyrat ship." Mr. Penn and others from the Jerseys said that Sulivan was an industrious man and very poor. He had a wife and three small children. Bellomont said that he had been "much solicited" to let Brown, Evans and Sulivan "have their liberty," but because he had no commission or direction from the king, he would not presume to set them free.[129]

4

LORD BELLOMONT'S WAR AGAINST THE PIRATES

L eonard Lewis deposed in May 1698 that his brother, "who had sailed with the pirate Tew in the Red Sea," asked for his advice about how he could escape trouble for his depredations. Lewis claimed that he went to Mr. Nicholas Bayard of the council, who advised him to go to Governor Fletcher. Lewis asked Fletcher to protect his brother. Fletcher answered that "a protection could not be obtained for less than one hundred dollars." When Lewis replied that his brother was poor, Colonel Bayard accepted seventy-five dollars, saying that he would try what he could do. Bayard, afterward, delivered to Lewis the protection signed by Colonel Fletcher. For his trouble, Lewis gave Colonel Bayard twelve pieces of Arabian gold. According to Lewis, a man named Samual Staats engaged in a similar transaction with Colonel Bayard.[130]

It was well known, apparently, that Colonel Fletcher had "admitted notorious pirates to bring their spoils into New York, receiving considerable rewards" for doing so. It was also no secret that a man named Mr. Nicoll had been the broker who made the bargain between Fletcher and the pirates, receiving 800 pieces of eight for his services. In May 1698, the Council of New York considered the depositions against Colonel Fletcher and agreed unanimously that Fletcher should be sent to the king. Nicoll acknowledged that he had received the money but that he "knew no pirates and had not acted as mediator between pirates and the governor but believed he was entitled to the said $800 for his pains." The council stated that Mr. Nicoll would be tried in the province rather than being sent to London.

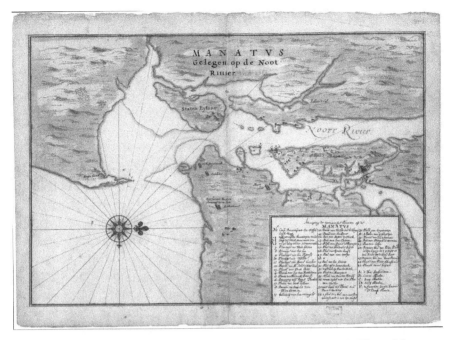

Manatus gelegen op de Noot [sic] Riuier, by Joan Vinckeboons, 1639. *Courtesy of the Library of Congress.*

The governor observed, however, that there was "such corruption in the government and such uproar if the law were enforced" that he would rather send both gentlemen home for trial. Mr. Nicoll was then ordered to give a security of £5,000 to appear when called on. The governor then suspended Mr. Nicoll from the council.[131]

Meanwhile, Governor Markham was again up to his ears in piracy complaints. Luke Watson and three of his compatriots reached out to Governor Markham on August 28, 1698, with a story to tell. Late one afternoon, a small ship and a sloop came to the capes, and they proved to be an enemy and French. The next morning, they landed about fifty well-armed men ashore and plundered nearly every house in the town, breaking open doors and chests and carrying off not only money, goods and merchandise but rugs and bed coverings as well. They left hardly anything in the place for cover or wear. The French pirates brought two bound English prisoners ashore with them; one of them was known to be the son of John Redwood of Philadelphia, so they supposed the sloop was his. The pirates then returned to the ship that night after killing several sheep and hogs, and they were still at anchor in the bay opposite the town, as close to shore as the water would let them. The men expected the pirates to land again the next day to kill more cattle or burn the houses. According to the men, the pirates lay ready for "all mischief inward or outward, by land or water." They were described as "beggarly rogues and will plunder for a trifle." The pirates took about eleven of the major townspeople prisoner, and after they had made the prisoners help ship their plunder, they released all of them except one. Pennsylvania, they argued, was in great danger and "very naked for defence."[132]

Governor Markham then wrote to Lord Bellomont, who, by this point, was well entrenched on the warpath against piracy, on September 2, 1698, to say that the pirates were "still about the capes" and that they had plundered a ship inward bound from Holland and chased a pink. The pink, he said, had come out of Rappahannock, bound for England, when the rogues took it and threw all its tobacco overboard, except for three hogsheads. The pirates waited for a vessel fit for their turn, as they were bound for the Red Sea, and "they have intelligence of one inward bound." Markham asked that Bellomont send the *Fowey* to cruise Pennsylvania's coast. Markham believed the *Fowey* could do as much service to New York as to Pennsylvania by sailing between Sandy Hook and Delaware's capes. The pirates took nine vessels, since they had come from the West Indies. Some of the prisoners whom the pirates released told their tales to Markham. According to him, the prisoners reported that there are no English on board the pirate ship, except two whom the pirates had impressed; there was only one Irishman, and the rest of them were French.[133] But Bellomont responded that he regretfully could not order either of the men-of-war to cruise for the pirates in Delaware Bay, as both were under orders for England, and he had no control over them. This meant that Pennsylvania was left to fend for itself against the pirates.[134]

Governor Quarry also sought advice on how to deal with pirates in his stead. In a letter from Quarry to Governor Nicholson, dated August 1698, he recalled that a sloop had recently come in from New York. It belonged to Mr. Moorhead, a Scotchman, and had approximately £1,000 worth of East India goods belonging to the pirates from Madagascar on board. Hearing of the sloop's arrival, the customs collector seized the sloop when it arrived in Newcastle. The customs collector took five barrels of "rich goods." As for "what bargain or composition he made for the rest, I know not." Quarry was later informed that the Newcastle customs collector had "embezzled and disposed of" the goods. Having done this, the customs collector admitted the sloop for entry and gave the merchant a certificate and a cocquet.[135] After all this, Quarry wrote to the collector of Philadelphia to seize the sloop,

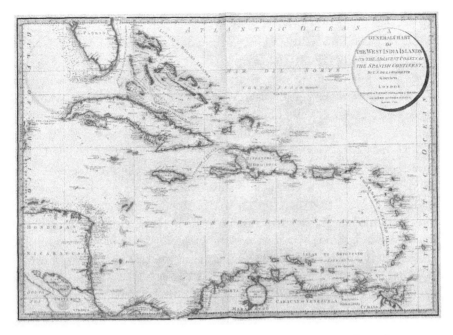

Islands of the West Indies, map by Louis Stanislaw de Larochette, 1796. *Image from Wikimedia Commons.*

which he did. The collector of Philadelphia then asked for Quarry's advice. Quarry told him that he should "seal the hatches, take the sails ashore, and put an officer on board," which he did. According to Quarry, he "never knew such roguery and folly." There was uproar in Philadelphia, however, that the last seizure was illegal, "since the sloop was admitted to entry and had her certificate." Quarry sought the advice of Nicholson, "the matter being none of my business 'til it comes before me judicially, nor can I hold a court without the officers."[136]

Perhaps the biggest thorn in the antipiracy governors' side was none other than Captain Kidd. He proved particularly troublesome to Bellomont, as he undermined Bellomont's war against the pirates. Kidd had long professed his innocence in the face of piracy accusations, arguing that he had been operating as a legally employed privateer. Kidd's proclaimed innocence on the charges of piracy were made all the more complicated with the depositions of Benjamin Franks, Nicholas Alderson and James How. They claimed that Kidd was a privateer who had "come out with a full power (which he showed me) to the East Indies to take pirates." But they alleged that he quickly turned to piracy. According to Frank, he lived in Barbados and Jamaica for several years, trading in several parts of the West Indies. But he lost £12,000 through the 1692 earthquake in Jamaica and as a result of enemy attacks. So, Franks decided to go to New York, where he met Captain Kidd. Franks opted to go with Kidd to catch pirates and remain wherever he could follow his profession as a jeweler. The men sailed from New York on September 6, 1696, in company with a Bermuda brigantine bound for Madeira. There, they met a Barbados brigantine and furnished it with some rigging and canvas, which it badly needed. A day or two afterward, they spied a ship, which they caught up with after three days' chase. The men found the ship to be a Portuguese ship heading from Brazil to Madeira. Captain Kidd exchanged presents with the captain. From Madeira, the men went to Bonavista and took in salt; then to St. Jago to take in water and provisions; and then they steered for the Cape of Good Hope. Before they reached the Cape of Good Hope, they met three English men-of-war and a fireship under the command of Captain Warren, who told the men that Kidd's commission was good and that he would not bother the men. Kidd promised to spare the commodore twenty or thirty men. A day or two after Kidd went on board one of the men-of-war, he returned "much disguised in drink" and left the squadron without furnishing the promised men. They headed straight for Madagascar, where they took in water and provisions at a place called Talleer. While there, a Barbados sloop came in, which followed them the whole way to Johanna and on to Mohilla, though Captain Kidd "told them several times to begone and back to Johanna." From there, they sailed for India and landed at a place called Motta, where the natives refused them water. So, Kidd sent two armed boats ashore, which seized provisions and six natives. Kidd also demanded and obtained two cows and two sheep as ransom. The four other prisoners escaped. From India, they went to the Babs and anchored to wait for pirates, but none came. But on August 17, ships came in, and Captain Kidd weighed and stood among them. The next morning, one of the fleets began to fire at Kidd and his men, at which point, they returned the favor. But after seeing English and Dutch colors, Kidd did all that he could to get away. Off the coast of St. John's, Kidd and his men met a small vessel under English colors. He chased and plundered it and afterward put into Carwar, where Franks gave Kidd a beaver to let him go ashore. According to Franks, most of Kidd's men seemed dissatisfied and anxious to escape.[137]

Nicholas Alderson corroborated much of Franks's testimony. Alderson deposed that he shipped himself with Captain Kidd when he learned that Kidd "was going to Madagascar as a privateer to put down the pirates"

Buried Treasure: Illustration of William "Captain" Kidd Overseeing a Treasure Burial, by Howard Pyle, pre-1911. *Image from Wikimedia Commons.*

and that if he could not find them there, he would proceed to India and the Red Sea to look for them. They waited at Babs for about four or five weeks to capture the pirates. At last, the Guzerat fleet came out from Mocha and, without acquainting any man of his design, Kidd chased after the fleet. But ultimately, he did nothing. The next morning, there was "little wind, and the fleet began to fire" at them. Captain Kidd, seeing English colors, immediately got out oars. The man-of-war, "for such she was," chased Kidd and his men. They escaped the ship and made for the highlands of St. Johns, which Alderson supposed was done to catch up to any stragglers from the fleet. They then "chased and plundered a ship under English colours." According to Alderson, the people were "tortured to make them confess where the money was, and the master was carried off to act as pilot." At Carwar, Alderson and eight other men, "finding ourselves to be on board a pirate, made our escape."[138]

Finally, James How claimed that he sailed from New York with Kidd in September 1696. They took, "without fight," a French company ship in the Indian Ocean and another commanded by Captain Wright, an Englishman, called the *Rambo Merchant*. Kidd and his men carried them to Madagascar and divided their lading. How said that from there, he decided to take passage to New York in the *Nassau*, which was owned by the notorious pirate trader and captain Giles Shelley. How further said that at St. Mary's, there was a great ship called the *Resolution*, whose crew had "forsaken her." Robert Culliver, who was one of these disaffected men, came on board the *Adventure Galley* and was "very intimate with Kidd." How said that while on the *Nassau*, he brought with him "200 pieces of Christian gold" for a man named Dickenson of Wethersfield in the colony of Connecticut, which was left to him by his son Obediah Dickenson, who had died in Madagascar.[139]

After receiving the men's testimony, Bellomont thought that this was "such an impertinence in both Kid [sic] and Livingston" that he had no choice but to arrest Kidd. Bellomont had noticed that Kidd "designed my wife a thousand pound in gold dust and ingots," but he "spoiled his compliment by ordering him to be arrested and committed that day," showing the council his orders from the court. Two gentlemen of the council, two merchants and the collector took charge of "all the cargoes," and they prepared inventories of everything that would be sent to the king immediately. Bellomont claimed that had he kept Mr. Secretary Vernon's orders to seize and arrest Kidd and his associates "with all their effects with less secrecy," he would have never gotten Kidd to come into port, "for his countrymen Mr. Graham and Livingston would have been sure to caution him to shift for himself and would have been well paid for their pains." After Kidd's arrest, Bellomont outfitted a ship to go in search of the *Quedah Merchant*. Bellomont had learned where the ship was via some papers that he had seized from Kidd and "by his own confession." According to Kidd's account of the cargo, Bellomont thought the ship was worth £70,000.[140]

The English East India Company was apprised of the piracies committed by Captain Kidd, whereupon circular letters were sent to all the American provinces by the secretary of state, commanding the governors there to "make search and seize him if he came within their reach." The first news of Kidd's return to America was a letter from the president and Council of Nevis to Mr. Secretary Vernon, dated May 18, 1699, and to the commissioners for trade, dated June 27, 1699. More news came from Lord Bellomont, who stated that it appeared Kidd had sailed from St. Thomas's for the Island of Mona, which lay between Puerto Rico and Hispaniola. While there, Kidd met with a pirate named Bolton of Antigua and the pirate Burt of St. Thomas's. Kidd sold them several goods and sent Bolton to Curaçao to fetch provisions for him. Having completed the task, Kidd gave Bolton a sloop and laded the best of his goods, sailing toward New York. He also entrusted the *Quedah Merchant* to Bolton. The next sighting of Kidd came from Colonel Quarry, the judge of the admiralty court in Pennsylvania, who wrote on June 6 that Kidd had arrived in Delaware Bay. From there, he sailed into the Sound of New York, sending word to his friends in New York.[141]

Lord Bellomont was so "fearful of the escape of the prisoners," because there were "no laws in that country for punishing piracy with death and that the people are so favourable to pirates that there could be no expectation of any justice against them there." So, the lord justices sent one of His Majesty's ships to fetch Kidd and the other pirates, bringing them "in safe custody together with their effects that had been seized" and the evidence against them so that they could be tried in England.[142] Meanwhile, the Council of Trade and Plantations wrote to the king "that unless Lord Bellomont be assisted by two able lawyers of known probity to supply the places of chief justice and attorney general, sent from hence, it will be impossible for him to perfect what he has begun in the reformation of those evil practices which had formerly taken root in the province of New York." By inviting "fit persons" and paying them £100 and £70 respectively, the colony may have hope of suppressing piracy and illegal trade.[143]

Kidd had been "hovering on the coast towards New York for more than a fortnight" and had asked a Mr. Emot from New York to meet him at a place called Oyster Bay in Long Island. Kidd then brought Emot to Rhode Island

and sent him to Lord Bellomont in Boston "with an offer of his coming into this part, provided I would pardon him." Bellomont stated that he "was a little puzzled how to manage a treaty of that kind with Emot, a cunning Jacobite, a fast friend of Fletcher's and my avowed enemy." When Emot proposed that Bellomont pardon Kidd, Bellomont told him that while it was true the king had allowed him a power to pardon pirates, he was loathe to use it, because he "would bring no stain on my reputation." Bellomont also claimed that he had a rule never to pardon piracy without the king's express orders. Emot told Bellomont that Kidd had left the great Moorish ship he took in India, the *Quedah Merchant,* in a creek on the coast of Hispaniola with goods valued at approximately £30,000. Further, Emot informed Bellomont that Kidd had bought a sloop, in which he had "several bales of East India goods, three score pound weight of gold in dust and in ingots, about a hundred weight in silver and several other things, which he believed would sell for about £10,000." Emot also told Bellomont that Kidd was "very innocent" and that his men had forced him to commit piracy by locking him up in the cabin of the *Adventure Galley* while they robbed two or three ships. Kidd claimed he could prove this with "many witnesses."

According to Bellomont, he said that if Kidd could, in fact, prove his innocence, "he might safely come into this port, and I would undertake to get him the king's pardon." So, Bellomont wrote a letter to Kidd, inviting him to come to port, and he assured him that Bellomont would "procure a pardon for him, provided he were as innocent as Mr. Emot said he was." Bellomont sent the letter to Kidd by way of Mr. Campbell, a resident of Boston and an acquaintance of Kidd's. Within three or four days, Campbell returned to Bellomont with a letter from Kidd, "full of protestations of his innocence and informing me of his design of coming with his sloop into this port." Campbell brought more than just the letter. Kidd had sent Campbell back with three or four small jewels to give to Bellomont's wife, which Bellomont claimed he knew nothing about. But once she apprised him of the situation and asked whether she should keep the jewels, Bellomont advised her to keep them until he had "made a full discovery what goods and treasure were in the sloop." Kidd landed in the port of Boston the next night, and Bellomont claimed he would not so much as speak with him unless there were witnesses. Bellomont thought Kidd looked "very guilty." Bellomont was certain of Kidd's guilt, because Kidd and his friends Livingston and Campbell began to "juggle together and imbezle some of the cargo" and that Kidd "did strangely trifle with me and the council three or four times that we had him under examination."

Kidd at Gardiner's Island: Illustration of Pirate Captain William Kidd's Supervision of the Burial of His Treasure at Gardiner's Island, by Howard Pyle, pre-1911. *Image from Wikimedia Commons.*

Mr. Livingston came to Bellomont preemptively, demanded his bond and told Bellomont that Kidd "swore all the oaths in the world that unless I did immediately indemnify Mr. Livingston by giving up his securities, he would never bring in that great ship and cargo but that he would take care to satisfy Mr. Livingston himself out of that cargo."

But Bellomont had more to worry about than Kidd. William Stoughton of Boston, a supporter of Lord Bellomont's antipiracy agenda, wrote to Secretary Vernon that around March 19, 1699, the *Adventure* of London arrived at the east end of Long Island, weighing about 350 tons with twenty-two guns. Thomas Gulleck was its commander, and the ship had sailed from Gravesend on March 16, 1698, bound for the island of Borneo in India. After an "interloping trade, being set forth by Capt[ain] Henry Tate and Capt[ain] Hammond, who keep a brewhouse in Thames Street," as well as Mr. Samuel Shepard and the Heathcotts, merchants in London, the ship proceeded to another location and stopped for water. While the commander and several of the officers, mariners and some passengers were on shore, and with the boats on board with water, the rest of the ship's company "combined and conspired together to leave them and run away with the ship and lading" on September 17. They cut the cable and brought the ship to sail, transporting those who didn't dare join them for their piratical venture to the shore. But they forced the surgeon's mate and two other youths to remain on board. The pirates were twenty-five or twenty-six in number and chose a man named Joseph Bradish, the boatswain's mate, to be their commander. They recognized his skill in navigation, and he directed their course for Mauritius, where they fitted the ship and took in some fresh provisions and two young gentlemen named Charles Seymore and John Power. From Mauritius, they came about Cape Bon Esperance, and a short time after that, they made "a sharing of the money on board, which was contained in nine chests stowed in the breadroom and set forth three or four and twenty single shares, besides the captain's, which was two shares and a half, weighing out the money." Some received $1,500, while others received $1,600 for a single share.

Afterward, they made a "second sharing of broadcloths, serges, stuffs and other goods on board." They stopped at Ascension Island, took some turtle and fresh provisions there and then directed their course for New York. They arrived at Long Island, where Captain Bradish went on shore, "carried the most of his money and jewels with him, committed them to the custody of a gentleman on the island and sent a pilot on board to remove the ship and bring her to an island called Gardiner's Island." Bradish's bag of jewels was recovered in New York. Allegedly, his treasure included "dozens of rings and pendants made of sapphires, rubies, emeralds, pearls, and diamond."[144] But the wind did not favor them, so they ran over to Block Island, within the realm of Rhode Island's government. At that point, they sent two men to Rhode Island to buy a sloop, but the government there, "having notice[d] that a ship was hovering about those parts suspected to be a pirate," seized the two men and detained them. News of this reached the pirate ship, and some sloops were described as coming from the island toward the ship. The pirates, fearing that they were outnumbered, came to sail and "stood off to seaward." But the sloops that were following them came upon them and stated that they wanted to trade with the pirates. So, the pirates permitted the men on the sloops to come on board. The pirates bought one of the sloops and hired another to transport them and their money. Meanwhile, the pirates allowed the sloopmen to take what they pleased out of the ship and, "having put their moneys on board the sloops, sank the ship and got on shore."[145]

They dispersed, "landing at farmhouses, where they provided themselves of horses and scattered into diverse parts of the country." The captain and some others who joined him went to New York. As soon as the news reached New York, Stoughton sent word "through the province and into the neighbouring government to pursue and seize all such of them as could be found, with their treasure." The captain and ten of his men were apprehended and placed into custody in Boston to await trial. The men, upon examination, confessed the particulars of their voyages and said that there was a considerable quantity of money—to the value of nearly £3,000. Stoughton seized several goods and the merchandise. Seven or eight more men were apprehended in Connecticut, and Stoughton continued to pursue the rest. The justices of the peace and other officers in their respective stations have been "very vigorous in the prosecution of these villains, and the people in general have a just resentment and abhorrence of such vile actions, and the government here [Boston] will be very zealous in the discountenancing and punishing of all such criminals."[146]

Additionally, Bellomont was still dealing with Colonel Fletcher's indiscretions. In February 1699, Lord Bellomont removed Colonel Thomas Willet from the council. According to Bellomont, Willet advised Colonel Fletcher's frequent embezzlement of revenue. Willet also advised and consented to a pirate bringing his ship and spoils into the port of New York and disregarded Fletcher's public acceptance of that ship as a present and of large sums for the protection of these and other pirates. Further, Willet concealed sums of money and treasure brought by known pirates from the Red Sea.[147]

Another of Fletcher's co-conspirators was Mr. Daniel Honan, who himself received bribes from pirates, granting them protections and committing other misdemeanors. While he was the private secretary to Fletcher, he provided security with other persons for two pirates on their setting out to sea. When the bonds were committed by Fletcher to his custody, Honan blotted out his own name in the body of the bonds and tore off his sign and seal at the bottom, leaving the names and seals of the other bondsmen untouched. When examined under oath by Lord Bellomont, he was asked whether he knew of any money that was given to or received by Fletcher for such protections. He swore that he knew of none. But it was later proven to Bellomont that he was present when Fletcher received a bill of fifty pounds for protection granted to one Rayner, a pirate. The bill was made payable to Honan himself for Fletcher's use, and he was accordingly paid. The Council of Trade and Plantations recommended that in case Honan should return to New York, he would not be protected by the king from any prosecution for these crimes.[148]

5

THE TROUBLE WITH COMPLICITY

In March 1699, Colonel Fletcher was brought to the Lords Justices in Council so that he could comment on "the complaints which had been made against him." There were eighteen total charges against him. Much of the evidence came from the depositions of Samuel Burgess and Edward Taylor. The minutes of the Council of New York, dated April 7, 1693, allegedly "prove the fact that the pirate crew were allowed the benefit of an act to which they were not entitled," but Fletcher, of course, denied this. So, too, did Colonel Bayard and Mr. Chidley Brook, "then of the council but since removed and now in England." The opinion of the Lords Justices was that "his proceedings, although with the consent of the council, were contrary to his duty and an encouragement to piracy." Fletcher admitted that "protections were granted and that gratuities might be paid to his servant" but not to known pirates, and he said that he did not receive any benefit. But the depositions of Samuel Staats and Thomas Lewis, as well as the admission of Bayard that Fletcher, "told him that upon application for protections, the persons concerned might make what presents they liked, confirm the charge." The Lords Justices did not believe that there was any "ground to believe that any security at all was ever taken when granting protections, and Colonel Fletcher admits no prosecutions were ever made of any such persons under what suspicion soever they lay." Based on this information and the deposition of John Wick, the Lords Justices were "humbly of opinion that, in granting such protections in the manner aforesaid, Colonel Fletcher gave great encouragement to pirates and neglected his duty in not causing such persons to be prosecuted."[149]

On the charge that Fletcher provided commissions to the pirates Tew, Glover and Hoar, Fletcher argued that this was done with "full approbation of the council and denies that he knew of their intentions to sail for the Indies and the Red Sea and, on the contrary, affirms that Tew made open vows never to go thither again." Allegedly, Tew posted the necessary £3,000 bond to support his commission as a privateer against the French and also paid Fletcher £300.[150] According to Bellomont, however, their intention of "sailing thither" was widely known to all in the province of New York. When it came to the charge that Fletcher was heavily involved with the pirate Tew, Colonel Fletcher stated that "this intimacy proceeded only from the pleasantness of his conversation and the information he thereby received about things observed by Tew in his voyages, together with his desire to reclaim Tew from an ill habit that he had got of swearing." As evidence, Fletcher said that he gave Tew a book and, "to gain the more upon him, also a gun of some value, in return whereof he received a present from him, which was a curiosity and in value not much."[151] But Tew allegedly met a grisly end. While trading at Madagascar, he joined forces with the infamous Henry Every, who wanted to capture the Mughal's fleet. Tew went after the *Fateh Muhammed*, one of the stragglers, but "a shot carried away the rim of his belly, and he held his bowels in with his hands some small space before he died."[152] His horrifying death so disturbed his crew that they quit chasing the *Fateh Muhammed*.

As for his commission of Thomas Moston, Fletcher acknowledged that he had granted the commission "upon the desire of several merchants who had hired the ship" to seize enslaved people from Madagascar but denied that he knew the ship was an "unfree bottom." But Bellomont stated that the ship was "known to all men to have been a former Dutch privateer and that the cargo she took in publicly at New York was goods proper for pirates." As evidence, they introduced that in the "charter party of affreightment," the ship was hired to lade "other goods," as well as enslaved people. According to the Lords Justices, the ship's seizure and confiscation for illegal trade on its return also supported the charge. Fletcher was also accused of taking securities against insolvency. The evidence with relation to the bonds given to Tew and Hoar consisted of the affidavits of Thomas Wenham, Joseph Smith, William Sharpass and Lancaster Symms. Fletcher laid the blame of the insufficiency of the securities and the tampering with the bonds on his servant Honan, whom he said he had "retained in his service that he may be forthcoming." On the aforementioned charges, the Lords Justices believed that though it did not appear that Fletcher knew that the persons to whom he had granted the commissions intended to go pirating, he should have used greater caution and sufficient security taken by the proper officers.[153]

Next, Fletcher was charged with willingly allowing illegal trade to take place in New York. The proof consisted of accounts and computations of the possibility of revenue. Fletcher and Bellomont submitted conflicting papers related to accounts of trade and revenue. Colonel Fletcher's generous land grants to prominent New York merchants and alleged pirate captains also came under scrutiny. Fletcher denied making any grants of land without the advice and consent of the council. According to him, it was the surveyor who was negligent and that the attorney general ought to be accountable for any faults in the grants. The "purchase" of the Mohawk people's land was, according to Fletcher, "fairly made." The Lords Justices were informed, however, that the attorney general was not consulted and was discharged from attending the council by Fletcher. They brought in Captain Evans, the former commander of HMS *Richmond*, for testimony. He gave the Lords Justices information concerning a grant made to him (which was estimated to have an area of forty miles by twenty miles) and assured them that the survey "was begun but could not have been perfected in six months." So, the Lords Justices felt that though it was left to Fletcher "by his instructions to make as large purchases of land as he could from the Indians for a small value," his large grants to individuals without "due caution for improvement was not for Your Majesty's service, nor did it tend to the settlement of those parts." The Lords Justices were "pleased, upon our [a]forementioned representation about the state of the province of New York," to direct Bellomont to put in practice "all methods whatsoever allowed by law for the breaking and annulling those exorbitant, irregular and unconditional grants."[154] Bellomont went one step further, believing many on board HMS *Richmond* to be pirates. Thus, he took the "opportunity to surprise and take a considerable number of" them, having "discovered the record of the pirates' commissions and of the bonds that they gave to Colonel Fletcher when he granted them commissions." The commissions appeared to be "so fraudulent that it is a proof that he was apprised of their design of piracy."[155]

Lastly, Fletcher was accused of subjecting his troops to miserable conditions, neglecting the province's fortifications, producing an illegal letter of "denization" and neglecting to notify the governor of Canada of the peace agreement. The Lords Justices appealed to the king to send the case to the attorney general to "consider and report what further proceedings may be had upon any of the [a]foresaid articles wherewith Col. Fletcher has been charged."[156]

As the evidence mounted against Governor Fletcher, the English Crown pondered who might replace him. It had to be an honest man who would not be so easily bribed. The Crown chose Lord Bellomont to succeed Fletcher after they recalled Fletcher to answer the charges leveled against him. Bellomont arrived in the colony of New York in 1697 and found the colony to be teeming with illicit commercial activity. Bellomont quickly became the most unpopular man in the colony, removing prominent officials who had been appointed by Fletcher. This included the removal of William Nicolls, Nicholas Bayard and Frederick Philipse from the governor's council. And despite repeated attempts to bribe Bellomont, he remained loyal to the Crown and the proclamation for the arrest of pirates.[157] Yet legal problems as a result of the pirates persisted. In 1699, the ability to try cases of piracy was granted to the colonies themselves. Royal instructions granted to Bellomont in 1701 demanded that he issue no privateer commissions unless the Crown expressly permitted him to. Therefore, authority in terms of maritime matters was centralized. By curtailing some of the governors' powers, the Crown further restricted the colonies.[158]

One major problem for Bellomont in his quest to eradicate piracy was the salaries granted to the new vice admiralty officials. It was well known that poorly paid officials were subject to accepting bribes or supporting other forms of illicit commerce. Generally, the court fees garnered from prize cases could make an individual a hefty income, but during times of peace, there were so few cases heard that the cases couldn't even cover general expenses. Around 1700, the judge's salary was fixed at £200 a year. This income was

By the king, a proclamation for the more effectual reducing and suppressing of pirates and privateers in America, 1687–88. *Courtesy of the Library of Congress, Jay I. Kislack Collection.*

directly drawn from the royal prizes or from the duties collected on prize goods. If that was insufficient, the funds would be drawn from other Crown income. This, in essence, made the court independent of the colony and made it much more difficult for the governors and other officials to influence its decisions by withholding stipends.[159]

Smarting from the problems that were undermining his antipiracy campaign, Lord Bellomont gave an update on the colony of New York to the Council of Trade and Plantations on May 3, 1699. According to him, five or six of the men who had run away with the ship under the command of Captain Bradish were also some of Colonel Fletcher's pirates who went out with Tew and other pirates commissioned by Fletcher. Two or three of them allegedly had wives in town and were actually there with their families. Bellomont tried to seize them, but "they are too well befriended to be given up to justice, and I am apt to believe they are still here." Bellomont informed the council about the deposition of John Clotworthy, the master of a sloop that had come to New York from Jamaica. Hyne (perhaps Hind), the pirate, was allegedly a "bloody villain, has murthered several men, and will give no quarter, they say, to Spaniards that he takes." According to Bellomont, Hyne "belongs to this town, his wife and family now here." He was supposedly master's mate of the *Fortune*, which Bellomont seized after his first arrival in New York; it was a ship that had also been commissioned by Fletcher. About three weeks later, a ship came in from Sandy Hook and lay at anchor for three days. The customhouse officer sailed by the ship in a sloop and hailed her, "asking whither she was bound; she answered to the Port of New York, but she never came hither, so that she is supposed to have been a pirate."[160]

In May 1699, Governor Blakiston of Maryland informed Secretary Vernon that he had received intelligence from Colonel Robert Quarry of Pennsylvania that there was a pirate off of Delaware Bay. But Quarry had been discouraged by the local government to apprehend them. As soon as Blakiston received Quarry's letter, he sent down a messenger to Governor Nicholson of Virginia, who had a man-of-war under his command. Blakiston asked Nicholson if they might send the man-of-war to seek out the pirates. Quarry also informed Blakiston that ten of the pirates were put on board a sloop from New York, bound for Virginia or Maryland; one was Gravenrod, the pirates' commander. So, Blakiston sent ships to all the places he thought he might capture the pirates. He got lucky when the pirates came into Severn River. Blakiston examined each of the men and "found them triffle, so various in their informations" that he seized their sloop and put them in prison. There were only six men in the sloop, so Blakiston concluded that they had disposed of the rest before landing. Five of them were known to belong to New York, and Blakiston greatly suspected one of them was a buccaneer. His name was Theophilus Turner, and during an examination, Turner told Blakiston that if he would save his life, he would "make an ingenious and genuine confession." In three separate depositions, Turner recounted how he had gotten out of England and come to be joined with those "knot of villains" who were also buccaneers. One Captain Shelley of New York brought them over from Madagascar. Turner further deposed how the pirates were "distributed here" and what vessels the other ten men had escaped in. Four had gone up Delaware Bay, while the rest had made haste for England. With this intelligence, Shelley, who brought the buccaneers, of which there were eighty or ninety, from Madagascar, was cleared from New York about ten months prior.[161]

The next month, on June 1, 1699, Colonel Quarry wrote to the Council of Trade and Plantations that approximately sixty pirates had lately arrived in Pennsylvania on a ship from Madagascar. He alleged that they were part of Kidd's gang. According to Quarry, about twenty had landed in Pennsylvania and sixteen had landed at Cape May. The ship lay near the cape of Pennsylvania, waiting for sloops from New York to unload it. Quarry believed it to be a very rich ship. Supposedly, "all her loading is rich East India bale goods and abundance of money." Quarry claimed that he had seized two of the pirates and had taken them to a jail in Burlington. He believed that if he had brought them before the current government, the pirates would have been "set at liberty, as Avery's [Every's] crew were." Quarry pursued two other pirates and kept them in Philadelphia. He informed Lieutenant Governor Markham and, with his assistance, placed them in prison. Then, Quarry said he "discovered their money and goods," which Markham took "into his hands and refuses to lodge them with the admiralty officers or to allow me to take an account of them." Quarry asked Markham to impress a vessel and raise forty men to seize the ship and "all in her." Markham refused. But Quarry did say that he had "2,000 pieces of eight, which I took from the two first pirates." He hoped the council would reimburse his charges from the loot.[162]

In a letter dated June 6, 1699, Quarry informed the council that, with Colonel Basse, the governor of the Jerseys, he had apprehended four more of the pirates at Cape May and "might have, with ease, secured all the rest of them and the ships, too, had this government [Philadelphia] given me the least aid or assistance." But the colony would not so much as issue a proclamation. On the contrary, "the people of this government have entertained the pirates, conveyed them from place to place, furnished them with provisions and liquors, given them intelligence and sheltered them from justice, and now, the greatest part of them are conveyed away in boats to Rhode Island." All the men who Quarry had hired to search for and apprehend the pirates were "abused and affronted and called enemies to the country for disturbing and hindering honest men, as they are pleased to call the pirates, from bringing their money and settling amongst them." Rather, according to Quarry, the act that the council passed against pirates and privateers contained no provision, like the Jamaica Act, that would make it a felony for the king's subjects to serve under any foreign prince against any other prince allied with His Majesty. The Jamaica Act had made all who knowingly entertained any person deemed or judged to be privateers and pirates accessories to piracy. But the Pennsylvania Act left out the word *deemed*, so when Quarry complained of accomplices, they answered that they did not know their acquaintances to be pirates until they were convicted. Jamaica's act empowered all commission officers, on notice of the arrival of any privateers or pirates, to raise however many men they saw fit to combat them. But the Pennsylvania Act omitted the word *armed* and empowered only the justices, sheriffs and constables to call men to their assistance. So, if the Quaker justices could "preach the pirates into submission, it is well." The clause that made it lawful to destroy pirates who resisted was left out, and the penalty for a man refusing to appear when called out was only a fine of five pounds. And Quarry's commission from the admiralty gave him no power to try piracy.[163]

Three days later, on June 9, 1699, Governor Basse wrote to William Popple, the secretary of the Board of Trade. He claimed that he had received no directions about the two pirates he had secured in East Jersey who were bailed out by Lord Bellomont. Both pirates were members of Every's crew, and one of them found to be "principally concerned in their horrid villainies." Basse also recounted how, on May 29, Captain Shelley, in the *Nassau*, had gone from New York to the island of St. Lawrence and arrived at Cape May in East Jersey. That evening, Shelley took on board Gravenrate (or Gravenrod) of New York.[164] Additionally, eight pirates had committed several hostilities in the Indies and made their voyage back to East Jersey with Shelley. Shelley had also landed fourteen men from St. Lawrence at Cape May; eight of them escaped with their effects before Basse learned of their arrival. Learning of their designs from Colonel Quarry, Basse "immediately manned out a sloop and, in person, went down to Cape May," where he took four of the persons suspected of piracy. The men confessed that they had been on the coast of India and had taken several prizes there.[165]

Dutch Men of War at Anchor, by Willem van de Velde I, circa the seventeenth century. *Courtesy of the Metropolitan Museum of Art.*

Two more of these men were taken with their effects on the river and were committed to the jail in Burlington. In their chests were about "7,800 Rix dollars and Venetians, about thirty pounds of melted silver, a parcel of Arabian and Christian gold, some necklaces of amber and coral [and] sundry pieces of India silks," which were all secured until Basse was informed of what to do with the prisoners.[166] Basse had no idea what the other four pirates carried with them. The pirates he had captured informed him that there were hundreds of men on the island of St. Lawrence who had gained considerable sums of money through robbery. They then wanted to retire and spend their ill-gotten wealth. Since the arrival of Shelley, Basse was informed that Captain Kidd was on a large sloop with about sixty men and that he had been seen between the two capes of Delaware. Basse complained that he had nothing beyond a "proprietary commission" to support him and that people seemed to desert him because of his refusal to approve of the pirates.[167]

Giles Shelley wrote to one "Mr. Delencie [Delancey], or, in his absence, Mr. John Barbarie, in New York." In his letter, dated May 27, 1699, Shelley stated that while at St. Mary's in Madagascar, he sold his goods from New York for "muslin, calicoes, a ton of elephants' teeth and two or three cwt. of opium."[168] He then took on board seventy-five passengers.

Twenty-four went ashore at Fort Dolphin, where Shelley claimed he bought a few enslaved people and some "pigs of tooth and egg." Most of the passengers were headed for Virginia and Horekill in Delaware with Andrew Gravenrod. Shelley claimed that for their passages, he had earned about 12,000 pieces of eight and about 3,000 Lyon dollars.[169] Shelley heard that there was no man-of-war in New York and designed to go to Sandy Hook. He remarked that Captain Burgess had arrived at St. Mary's the day he sailed for North America and that Burgess, too, had sold his goods very well.[170] According to Bellomont, Shelley "has so flushed 'em at N[ew] York with Arabian gold and E[ast] India goods, that they set the government at defiance," bringing in upward of £50,000 in money.[171]

6

THE PIRATES' RECKONING

Bellomont frequently complained of the abuses suffered at the hands of pirates and the unscrupulous merchants who supported them. In a letter to the Council of Trade and Plantations in August 1699, Bellomont remarked that he "tendered the bill for punishing privateers and pirates, but it would not go down with the council [in Boston], especially the clause which declares piracy felony and punishable with death." He argued with the council that it would be best for them if all their laws conformed with those of England. At this insistence, "three or four councillors stood up at once, and one or two asked me with some warmth what the laws of England had to do with them." One of the councilors argued that "they were too much cramped in their liberties already and they must pass for great fools should they abridge the liberty that was left 'em by an act of their own." Bellomont was aghast at their remarks and relayed to the Council of Trade and Plantations that "pirates multiply very much and will endanger a total loss of the trade from England to the East Indies unless speedily suppressed," which couldn't happen so long as the colonial governors and councilors, like those in New York and Pennsylvania, remained dishonest and inactive. Bellomont then gave the example of Colonel Webb, the former governor of Providence Island, who was robbed in the James River while he went ashore at Newcastle, Pennsylvania, to refresh himself. The crew sailed away with his ship and all his estate, amounting to £7,000 in gold and £1,000 in goods. According to Bellomont, if you were to ask Colonel Webb how he amassed £8,000 in two years in such a "paltry island," Bellomont believed Webb would say he "but trod in the steps of his predecessor, Trott, the greatest pirate broker that ever was in America." The attorney general of Barbados Mr. Hooper told Bellomont that Trott could "not have got less than £50,000 by pirates and that he had cunningly dispersed his money in Barbadoes, New York and Boston." Bellomont believed the pirates "need no other sanctuary; there, they are furnished with provisions and all things else for their purpose brought thither from the other plantations."[172]

And Bellomont got what he asked for. The Lords Justices in the council sent orders to "the Earl of Bellomont, Mr. Penn or the governor-in-chief of Pennsylvania and the governor of East and West New Jersey that all persons that have been or shall be seized for piracy in the provinces of Massachusetts Bay, New York, New Hampshire, Pennsylvania or in East or West New Jersey be sent over hither in safe custody, together with all money, goods or other effects seized with them and all such evidences as may be of any use for their conviction."

Bellomont also sent orders to his lieutenant general in New York to apprehend the masters of the sloops that "conveyed bales of goods from Kidd's sloop towards New York." As a result, Bellomont was able to recover some of the goods, which were sent to Boston. Bellomont was suspicious,

Naues Mercatoriæ Hollandicæ per Indias Occidentales (Dutch East Indiaman), map by Wenceslaus Hollar, 1647. *Courtesy of the Metropolitan Museum of Art.*

though, that Mr. Gardiner had not sent all that Kidd had left with him. For example, "one Syms of New York took away" one of the enslaved boys left by Kidd with Gardiner. There was also a rumor about a waistcoat of Kidd's with diamond buttons that was concealed. After searching diligently, Bellomont found the waistcoat, "but the stones were plainly Bristol stones tho' set in gold. I believe Kidd thought they were right diamonds by his conveying the waistcoat away in the manner he did."[173] According to the deposition of William Kidd, his chest, "which he left at Gardner's Island," included three small bags "or more of Jasper Antonio or stone of Goa, several pieces of silk stript with silver and gold cloth of silver, about a bushell of cloves and nutmegs mixed together and strawed up and down, several books of fine white calico, several pieces of fine muslins, several pieces more of floured silk" and more, which Kidd could not recall. Kidd had an invoice of his other chest. According to Kidd, "all that was contained in the said chest was bought by him and some given him at Madagascar, nothing thereof was taken in the *Quedah Merchant*. He esteemed it to be of greater value than all else that he left at Gardiner's Island, except the gold and silver; there was neither gold or silver in the chest. It was fastened with a padlock and nailed and corded about." Kidd further said that he had left a bundle of nine or ten fine India quilts, some of them silk with fringes and tassels, at Gardiner's Island.[174]

In October 1699, Bellomont prevailed upon seizing and sending Thomas Clark of New York to England as a prisoner. According to Bellomont, Clark had been on board Kidd's sloop at the east end of Long Island and had "carried off about £5,000 in goods and treasure, and perhaps more, into Connecticut Colony" and, thinking himself safe from Bellomont's authority, wrote to Bellomont's lieutenant general a "very saucy letter and bade us defiance." Bellomont ordered him to be kept in the fort, because the prison was weak and insufficient. Bellomont stated that when orders would come to him to send Kidd and his men to England, "which I long for impatiently," he would send Clark as an associate of Kidd's. He sent Clark's proposal that Clark would "surrender all the goods and treasure he received" to the lieutenant general and advised them that he would become Clark's advocate if he actually released his loot. The lieutenant general replied that Clark offered £12,000 in "good security and will, on oath, deliver up all the goods he hath been entrusted with from Kidd, provided he may go and fetch them."[175] So Bellomont directed the lieutenant general "to take the £12,000 security offered and his oath to the punctual performance of what he has proposed."

Meanwhile, Paroculus Parmyter wrote to Lord Bellomont from New York in a letter dated September 25, 1699. According to Parmyter, he seized a ship for illegal loading, which came from Jamaica and was owned by Mr. Wenham and Robert Allison, a man who was famous in his time for his piratical depredations. But Parmyter had no "great hopes to get judgment, as things are carried on," given the nature of trade in New York. Another vessel escaped. Parmyter also arrested Adolphus Phillips, one of the owners of the escaped ship.[176]

As Bellomont continued his war against the pirates, he relied on the assistance and compliance of the mid-Atlantic governors. In the minutes of the Council of New York from August 1699, advertisements were ordered to be published for the apprehension of Gilliam the pirate. Additionally, the high sheriffs of King's and Queen's Counties were ordered to seize Humphrey Clay, Martin Schank and John Harrison, who were pirates from Kidd's ship. All the goods that were seized and brought into the Custom House were ordered to be kept there until they were discharged by order of the board or by due course of law.[177] Also in August, Colonel Basse, the governor of the Jerseys, "got some pirates with a good store of money at Burlington" in West Jersey. Bellomont heard they were Kidd's men, too. All these pirates were brought from Madagascar by Giles Shelley and were "a good many of 'em Kidd's men that forsook him and went on board the *Mocha* frigate."[178] Governor Basse remarked that Shelley had arrived with the pirates and "£50,000 on board."[179]

In November 1699, Bellomont wrote to the Council of Trade and Plantations again, this time with a story of his apprehension in Boston of the pirate Gilliam, also known by the name of James Kelly. Gilliam was wanted for the murder of Captain Edgecomb, the commander of the *Mocha* frigate of the East India Company, as well as for his piracies committed with Captain Kidd. Gilliam was allegedly the man who encouraged the ship's company to become pirates, and the ship "has been ever since robbing in the Red Sea and seas of India." According to the reports Bellomont had received from men coming in from Madagascar, Gilliam and his crew had taken more than £2,000,000 sterling. In addition to seizing Gilliam, Bellomont also arrested Francis Dole, whose house Gilliam was harbored in. Dole was allegedly one of Hoar's crew, one of Fletcher's pirates, commissioned by him from New York.

According to Bellomont, his "taking of Gillam was so very accidental, one would believe there was a strange fatality in that man's stars." Bellomont clearly had a flair for the dramatic. Gilliam was allegedly a member of Kidd's crew for some time and thus had strong connections to New York. Bellomont seized four pounds of gold from Gardiner's Island. Additionally, he seized all the jewels that belonged to Gillam. Bellomont argued that, as vice-admiral of these provinces, he was entitled to one-third of Gillam's gold and jewels, and he hoped the king would reward him accordingly. At the same time that he seized Gilliam and Dole, Bellomont took one of the pirates who had been brought from Madagascar by Shelley of New York, signed by Governor Jeremiah Basse of West and East Jersey. Basse allegedly took several pirates at Burlington in West Jersey, who each had a "good store of money with them."

In November 1699, Shelley was further accused of bringing the pirate Sion Arnold from Madagascar to West Jersey, signed off by Governor Basse, which was a bold step for Basse after he received such positive orders from Secretary Vernon. But Bellomont claimed he "perceive[d] plainly the meaning of it, he took several pirates at Burlington in West Jerzey and a good store of money with them," and "dare say, he [Basse] would be glad they [should] escape, for when they [the pirates] are gone, who can witness what money be seized with 'em?" According to Bellomont, he knew Basse so well that he "verily believe[d] that's his plot."[180]

Yet even the upstanding and loyal Lord Bellomont was at one point charged with colluding with pirates—first in February 1700. Jeremiah Basse, the former governor of East Jersey, had seized two men in East Jersey: John Elston and William Merrick, who confessed themselves to have been members of Every, the pirate's, crew. Basse claimed he had refused to bail them out, but Bellomont "by a pretended admiralty power, forced them out of his hands and set them at liberty upon insufficient bail." Merrick was able, thus, to make his escape.[181] Bellomont was accused again in December 1700. His charge? That he knowingly allowed the *New York Marchand* to come to New York after having been in Madagascar. According to Bellomont, however, he inquired about the ship and stated that he had learned Frederick Philipse was the ship's owner. Philipse had appointed the ship to stop at Delaware Bay, fifty leagues west of New York, where his son met the ship in the *Fredericks'* sloop. Philipse's son took out all the East India goods and sent the *Fredericks'* sloop and its goods to Hamborough. He then came to New York City in the *New York Marchand*. After receiving notice that the ship was coming in, Bellomont claimed he immediately searched the ship, but there was nothing found except a "parcel" of enslaved people. The trade of enslaved people to Madagascar was not then prohibited, so Bellomont felt he had no case against the ship. He defied "all mankind to charge me justly with any sort of corruption in the least degree, or with any connivance or partiality shew'd to one man or party more than another."[182]

Although piracy in the mid-Atlantic was facing a reckoning, pirates continued to haunt the region in the eighteenth century. In April 1700, William Penn wrote to the Council of Trade and Plantations that a man named James Brown, a planter in Pennsylvania, claimed only to have been a passenger in Henry Every's ship—so indeed said two of Every's crew, Chinckton and Lacy. It also came to Penn's attention that when Captain Kidd was off the capes of Pennsylvania, near Lewes, Delaware, that George Thomson, Peter Lewis, Henry Stretcher, William Orr and Diggory Tenny had gone on board Kidd's ship. Thomson, Lewis and Stretcher allegedly stayed on board for twenty-four hours, while Orr and Tenny were only there for an hour. But all the men brought goods, such as "calico, silk, muslin, sugar, and their loot," on shore, valued at approximately £300, which they concealed and sold. It was also believed that Kidd's men had received the equivalent of £4,000 as their share of the loot. Thomson, Lewis and Orr were under suspicion of being old pirates, whose compatriots "have long sown themselves in Boston, Road Island, New York, Jersey, Pensilvania, Maryland, Virginia and Carolina, where their capt[ain], one Reiner, now lives." Colonel Quarry informed Penn that he had bought their ship. There were eighty-four men on the crew. Five of them stayed in Pennsylvania. Three of them decided to embark on a "life of husbandry, turning planters," while the other two "have trades." The men claimed they didn't know it was Kidd but believed him to be a man named Samuel Wood, "who, with four men, came on shore to mend an iron belonging to the boom of the sloop." These men asserted that they had come from Antigua and were bound for Philadelphia with sugar, rum and molasses.[183]

Penn examined Thomson, Lewis, Stretcher, Orr and Tenny, all of whom were then in jail there. They pleaded their willingness to do anything for money, "after being plundered, as was all the town, by a French privateer but a year before." The men said they were ignorant of any proclamation against Kidd and that they had the goods of Samuel Wood and "one Gillam and that it was not purchase but gift." The men offered to deliver up the goods they had—or at least the value of them—and "give good security to behave well." They were poor, married men who had children, but, according to Penn, "such men must not be endured to live near the seacoasts nor trade, lest they become receptacles and broakers for younger pirates." The then-present laws in Pennsylvania "will hardly reach them, looking only forward for such as commerce with pirates." The general assembly would by no means seize alleged pirates, "lest honest people might be affected, since many of those reputed pirates had, some years ago, been permitted to live in

Capture of the Galleon, by Howard Pyle, 1887. *Image from Wikimedia Commons.*

this and other provinces, on condition that they left them not without leave and behaved well while they staid." Penn awaited the king's orders, placing all the men "good bonds, and so suffer them to live with their families on their plantations" until he received further directions.[184]

Meanwhile, Colonel Quarry informed the Council of Trade and Plantations in June 1700 that he "had then a prospect of seizing all the pirates and their effects," valued at £30,000, which he would have successfully seized had he not been "betrayed by some ill men of these governments, who gave the pirates intelligence and carried them off the country in boats."[185]

The following year, in December 1701, George Larkin informed the Council of Trade and Plantations that two pirates who had been convicted with Kidd, How and Churchill, had lately returned from England to Pennsylvania. He was "credibly informed" that the two men had retrieved £1,500 (How) and £800, "which they had buried in the woods when they first landed." Larkin further observed that the pirates had been "hugged and caressed after a very strange manner by the religious people of those parts, no money to be seen amongst them now but Arabian gold." Additionally, Larkin remarked that the "proprietary governments are very prejudicial to the king's interest, they are a sort of a recepticle or refuge for pyrates and unlawful traders." There was "scarce a family in three" that wasn't in some way connected to "privateering" as the locals called it. And a great many were involved in Pennsylvania and the Jerseys.[186]

After remaining in Philadelphia for only three days, Larkin made his way through the Delaware Bay and into East Jersey. He found the political situation there quite dire. For example, in March 1701 in Monmouth County, court was being held to determine the fate of one Moses Butterworth, who had confessed his role in Captain Kidd's last voyage to the East Indies. Governor Andrew Hamilton and his men had rushed to the courthouse to try Butterworth, hoping to quickly and publicly reassert their authority over the local population, who had knowingly protected pirates for years. But Samuel Willet, a local leader, thought that the governor and his justices didn't have the authority to hold an admiralty court. So he sent Thomas Johnson to "sound the alarm" and gather together a group of armed men to break up the court proceedings. Johnson led the militia to the courthouse, where they broke into the courtroom where Butterworth was being tried, making such a ruckus that it was impossible to examine Butterworth and his connections to Kidd and the local gentry. Two brothers, Benjamin and Richard Borden, seized Butterworth while the judge and sheriff attempted to put an end to the shenanigans. According to later examinations, there were more than one hundred "furious locals" who took Hamilton, the sheriff and the justices and imprisoned them until Butterworth was cleared of all charges and freed. Thus, Butterworth seems to have been freed, heading to Newport, Rhode Island, where, in 1704, he turned in his pirate hat for a sloop to pursue deserters and men who turned to piracy.[187]

By this point, Virginia, and especially Maryland, were indignant at the report that illicit trade and piracy alike were openly supported by William Penn's deputy in Philadelphia. But it's important to note that Virginia and Maryland were "furiously jealous" of Pennsylvania's thriving trade and prosperity and that Maryland had actually imposed special duties to damage Pennsylvania's trade. Governor Nicholson of Virginia had even sent an armed party over the Pennsylvanian border to arrest some men who were accused of piracy. Maryland and Virginia's governors were not necessarily wrong in their suspicions. There was abundant evidence that Governor Markham in Philadelphia had given his blessing not only to illegal trade but to piracy as well and that he did so with "little to no concealment." With great ingenuity, the assembly of Pennsylvania tried to legitimize this illicit traffic by removing the question of trade from the jurisdiction of the king's officers. But the government's defense of itself against the charges

Morgan at Porto Bello, by Howard Pyle, 1888. *Image from Wikimedia Commons.*

of Edward Randolph and others was not very convincing. Moreover, in spite of all warnings, Pennsylvanians persisted in illicit commerce and in aiding and abetting pirates because of the "oppressive nature" of the 1696 Navigation Acts. Merchants like Gerard G. Beekman, recognizing that the slim difference between profit and loss depended on their compliance with the Navigation Acts, often resorted to evasive measures, such as "bribing customs collectors, doctoring ships' manifests, circulating fraudulent bond certificates, and outright smuggling." These activities became a way of life after the passage of the Molasses Act in 1733.[188]

The Council of Trade, however, was not disposed to ignore this defiance of imperial authority. Among the provisions of the Navigation Acts (1696) was a clause that the governors of proprietary colonies must take an oath to execute the Acts of Trade and that their appointments would not be valid unless confirmed by the king. This clause had been generally evaded by the colonies, but the House of Lords passed a resolution that security would be required of the proprietors themselves for the good behavior of their chosen governors. Generally, Penn was inclined to excuse his agents for all their malpractices, because they increased the wealth of the settlement and, presumably, added to his own wealth.

RUMOR, INTRIGUE AND THE DECLINE OF PIRACY IN THE EIGHTEENTH CENTURY

E ven Blackbeard was known to haunt the Delaware Bay, despite making the Carolinas and the Caribbean his main targets. In 1718, Blackbeard blockaded Charleston, South Carolina, where he held many prominent men hostage until the governor agreed to send back medical supplies that Blackbeard could use to treat his ill and dying men, particularly those suffering from syphilis. The governor, well aware of Blackbeard's reputation, sent the requested medical supplies, and true to his word, Blackbeard released the hostages—but not before he stripped them of nearly all their clothing and personal effects. After the blockade, Blackbeard made his way up the coast, to New Jersey's Little Egg Harbor. He allegedly made one of the numerous little islands behind Brigantine Island a temporary camp, where he could hideout. For the next few weeks, he sailed along the New Jersey coastline. Blackbeard was also rumored to have buried a vast amount of his loot in Burlington, New Jersey, and was believed to have stayed at the Marcus Hook Plank House Log Cabin in Pennsylvania, where a young woman, who may have been one of his alleged fourteen wives, often took care of him.[189]

A rumor emerged that the British had mounted a massive search for Blackbeard and that they had found his hideout and chased him all the way into the Jersey swamps. It is unclear how true this particular story is, but Blackbeard nonetheless had decided to leave the Delaware Bay, at which point, he beached and sank the *Queen Anne's Revenge* as he made his way southward. He ultimately met a grisly end, as Lieutenant Robert Maynard was sent to stamp out Blackbeard's depredations. Legend has it

An illustration of Blackbeard's Jolly Roger flag. *Image from Wikimedia Commons.*

that Maynard caught up to Blackbeard near Ocracoke Island and that a shouting match took place between the two men. According to Captain Charles Johnson in his salacious *A General History of the Pyrates*, Blackbeard "took a glass of liquor, and drank to him with these words: 'Damnation seize my soul if I give you quarters, or take any from you.'"[190] Fighting broke out, and Blackbeard "received a shot into his body from the pistol that Lieutenant Maynard discharg'd, yet he stood his ground, and fought with great fury, 'til he received five and twenty wounds, and five of them by shot." Reportedly, Blackbeard "was cocking another pistol, having fired several, before he fell down dead." Then Maynard caused Blackbeard's head "to be severed from his body, and hung up at the bolt-sprit end." After Blackbeard's death, as Maynard's crew rummaged through his ship, they allegedly found letters and papers revealing correspondence between Blackbeard and "some traders at New York."[191]

Another infamous pirate who was alleged to have visited the mid-Atlantic was Bartholomew "Black Bart" Roberts. While little to no evidence exists to suggest Roberts sailed the Delaware Bay, it hasn't stopped rumor and legend from taking root. According to one of these legends, in the summer of 1720, Roberts was high off a series of successful ventures and attacks and decided to make his way southward from Newfoundland. He made for Virginia's waters, where he captured a merchant vessel and decided to make his mark near Charleston, South Carolina. Unfortunately, a major storm forced him back northward, where he and his crew, split among the *Royal Fortune* and *Good Fortune*, managed to allegedly dock at Cape May in New Jersey. But his reputation preceded him, and local ships gathered together to seize Roberts, while the Royal Navy blockaded the port to prevent the pirates' escape. Roberts and his men were surrounded, but that didn't stop them from attempting a brazen escape. Unfortunately, Robert's ship the *Royal Fortune* was hit with so many shots that it could no longer remain afloat. As the ship sank, the crew and Roberts swam to the *Good Fortune*, where they managed to escape the mêlée. They left behind the *Royal Fortune* and all the gold, silver and other valuables within it, which supposedly remain sunk beneath the waters of the Delaware Bay, somewhere off Cape May.[192]

From that point onward, references to piracy in the mid-Atlantic become scant. But in a letter from Governor Burnet to Lord Carteret, he provided the good news that a New York station ship, under the command of Captain Solgard, had, on June 10, 1723, engaged two pirate sloops at once. There were about seventy men and eight guns on each ship, each of which were under the command of the pirate Low. Having disabled one ship that evening, Solgard lost sight of the other ship, "which seem'd much shattered." So he brought his prize into Rhode Island and immediately went out in search of the other. According to the letter, Solgard had intelligence that he could find the other pirate ship east of Boston.[193]

In 1782, a pirate named Thomas Wilkinson was hanged for his crimes on Windmill Island, off the coast of Philadelphia. It was a known pirate haunt, and several pirates were hanged there.[194]

There are several reasons why piracy declined in the mid-eighteenth century, especially in the mid-Atlantic. One reason was the issuing of new acts or statutes that influenced the choices of individual pirates. The Act of Grace, issued by King George in September 1717, with a follow-up pardon opportunity in 1719, had mixed results. But the Crown also provided an

Real pirate treasure at the Houston Museum of Natural Science. *Image from Wikimedia Commons.*

incentive for the apprehension of or information that led to the capture of a pirate: £100 for a pirate captain; £40 for "officers" or important pirates, such as lieutenants, masters, boatswains, carpenters and gunners; £30 for lower-ranking officers; and £20 for other crew members. There was even an incentive for a pirate to turn their captain in: £200.[195] In 1721, the Crown supplemented the Act for the More Effectual Suppression of Piracy (1700) with a statute that not only reiterated the penalty of death for anyone convicted of piracy or of being an accessory to piracy but also required all members of an armed merchant ship to fight back

The Pirates and the Parrot, by Cecil Glossop, 1930. *Image from Wikimedia Commons.*

against pirates if attacked. They would face being stripped of their wages and imprisoned for six months if they did not fight back. Additionally, this statute increased the penalties for any naval officer who was caught trading with pirates. Those who were caught would face a court-martial, where, if convicted, they would lose their position, be denied any wages they were due and would be barred from serving in the navy in the future.

A second reason for the decline in piracy after 1719 was the increased presence of British warships along the colonial coast. Third, pirates lost their base of operations in New Providence, where they would often hide, refit and refuel or trade. Fourth, and perhaps most importantly in terms of the decline of piracy along the mid-Atlantic coast, was the changing attitude of the American colonists. As we have seen, in the mid- to late 1600s, pirates were generally welcome by the colonists and even the government. Pirates not only brought commodities that the colonists greatly desired and needed, but they also infused the local economy with significant amounts of cash. Furthermore, pirates' targets were typically Mughal ships in the Indian Ocean or Spanish ships in the Caribbean, which seemed beneficial to the colonists and with little risk. But by 1716, pirates were no longer bringing in valuable commodities or loads of cash as a result of the War of the Spanish Succession and the general collapse of the Mughal empire's wealth. Instead, the pirates turned to attacking British and American vessels, damaging local economies rather than supplementing them. According to historian Eric Jay Dolin, "No longer were pirates the much-beloved fathers, brothers, and friends of colonists who enriched their communities, but rather, they were outsiders who, for the most part, brought nothing but strife."[196] By this time, the colonies were actually quite a bit more prosperous than they had been in the seventeenth century, which meant they had more to protect from the pirates they now viewed as a threat.

As efforts to eradicate piracy in the Atlantic witnessed increased successes, the number of pirates continued to dwindle. By the time William Fly was hanged and gibbeted in 1726, an event that many mark as the end of the golden age of piracy, there were so few pirates left that they no longer threatened commerce in the Atlantic World. The governors and residents of the mid-Atlantic no longer needed the pirates to support their economy; instead, they turned their attention to more profitable (and legal) ventures, like shipbuilding, timbering, textile manufacturing, printing and publishing and agriculture.

PART II

DO YOU DESIRE FORTUNE OR REVOLUTION?

I think experience has shewn that privateers have done more towards distressing the trade of our enemies and furnishing these states with necessaries than continental ships of the same force, and that is, in my opinion, the greatest advantage we can, at present, expect.

—Josiah Bartlett to William Whipple, June 20, 1778

8

FROM PIRATE TO PRIVATEER

lthough the golden age of piracy may have ended in 1726, pirates—who would later operate technically as privateers—had not totally vanished. Prior to the American Revolution, privateering proved to be quite profitable to the mid-Atlantic colonies, especially during King George's War (1744–48) and the French and Indian War (1754–63). During King George's War, for example, over three dozen privateers out of New York alone operated in the Caribbean. They seized several hundred French and Spanish ships valued at £168,000, which was divided among the privateers and their investors. One of the most prolific of these privateers was the *Royal Hester*, which seized no fewer than forty prizes worth more than £63,800. Approximately seven other privateers generated a revenue of more than £40,000, and Captain Peter Warren managed to secure a single French merchantman carrying £9,000 worth of indigo and sugar.[197]

During the French and Indian War, more than seventy privateers operated out of New York alone. It was considered the "greatest such fleet by far in the colonies." And they were immensely successful, bringing in more than six hundred prizes worth more than £1.4 million. Between September 1756 and May 1757, several prizes worth more than £200,000 arrived in New York City. Privateers seized everything from coffee and sugar to wine and pottery, dry goods and lumber to enslaved peoples. They also obtained countless quantities of hard specie, including gold doubloons, French louis d'or and Spanish pieces of eight. The *Royal Hester* once again proved to be one of the most prolific privateers, bringing in twenty-five prizes valued at

£115,000. Between 1739 and 1763, "legalized plunder poured something like" £2 million into the coffers of approximately two hundred investors. This was an outrageous accumulation of wealth during a period in which an income of £300 was enough to live "like a gentleman" in New York, according to merchant Gerard G. Beekman.[198]

Not everyone made as much profit, if any, in these ventures. Generally, a privateer crew signed on for up to 60 percent of the value of the prize. A seasoned captain might receive an extra £200 to £300 for his services on a voyage lasting nine to twelve months. A privateer crew that returned with approximately £35,000 in prizes would ultimately have somewhere between £12,000 and £21,000 to split between them. And with a crew of around seventy-five men, they might earn around £160 and £280 each. This was a lot of money, considering that the common laborer earned only £30 annually. But between the multitude of "contractors, suppliers, and lawyers to be paid, not to mention the costs to be absorbed when a ship returned empty-handed or didn't return at all," some shareholders lost everything or barely covered their expenses. And most privateers came home empty-handed, if they came home at all. On average, one out of every two or three men was either killed, captured or injured. But as a whole, merchants did well enough that they could reasonably expect to make double or even triple their money within a year or less. For example, Christopher Bancker outfitted his merchantman as a privateer in 1744. It cost him £1,200. In the meantime, he earned some profit by selling shares of the venture to seven other merchants and captains. His privateers made three cruises and captured prizes valued at more than £42,400. Once the crew received their share and all other expenses were covered, each investor earned approximately £1,800, which was a 140 percent return on investment. Privateering was so popular in places like New York, despite the risks, that shipowners often had to offer five shillings a day (three times the peacetime rate) to assemble a good crew.[199]

The prosperity brought in by the privateers enabled other vocations to flourish and created an economic boom in New York City. The shipyards of the East River, for example, did so much business refitting merchantmen with the requisite cannon and sail to manage a Caribbean venture and repairing those that returned to port, that ropemakers, sailmakers, coopers and chandlers all had steady employment. Additionally, the presence of privateers and military or naval officers aided in a construction boom, increasing the number of homes in New York from 1,991 in 1753 to nearly 2,600 by 1760. This provided steady employment for "bricklayers, stonemasons, glaziers, plasterers, painters, and carvers," who could command wages that were 25

New York Harbor, by Fitz Henry Lane, circa 1855. *Image from Wikimedia Commons.*

percent higher than those received in peacetime. Merchant shops thrived on the increased demand for "wines, tobacco, china, glassware, stationery, and teas."[200] Much of the retailing was done by women, "widows, as well as the wives of merchants and sea captains," and some did so well that they "crossed the line separating shopkeepers from she-merchants." For example, Martha Carrick, who ran an ordinary shop until 1761, began operating in the storehouse of a former merchant and selling wholesale. And Frances Willett on Wall Street was able to sell sugar and rum by the hogshead, "which she fetched from St. Kitts on her own two ships."

But the most successful of these wartime retailers, particularly among the privateers, were the tavern owners. They sold food and drink and often provided lodging for the thousands of seamen who passed through the city each year. New York had more licensed public houses than any other colonial city. There were 334 in 1752, up from 166 in 1744. And many of the merchants who had once imported spirits, like rum, began making their own. There were ten rum distilleries in the city in 1753.[201] It's important to note that this prosperity, bred by the privateers, had a significant impact on the number of enslaved people in the mid-Atlantic colonies, especially in New York. For example, in 1756 there were 695 enslaved Black women over the age of sixteen and 443 under the age of sixteen serving the 10,800 white people who lived in the city. Enslaved Black men were forced to do much of the city's hard labor, including working as fishermen, coopers, barbers and boatmen.[202]

9

THE REVOLUTION COMES
TO THE MID-ATLANTIC

On May 26, 1776, a British warship, the *Asia*, arrived at the East River, inflaming political tensions and dividing the loyalties of New York residents.[203] Those tensions mounted until, on August 27, 1776, more than thirty-two thousand British regulars, 10 ships of line, 20 frigates and 170 transport vessels defeated Washington's troops at Kip's Bay and invaded Manhattan. New York was officially under British occupation by the end of the month. While it may have seemed like the British occupation would destroy the economy of the city, superficially, it actually restored some of the 1750s prosperity that the city had enjoyed—at least for the tens of thousands of Loyalists who fled other colonies for New York. During occupation, Parliament issued the authorization for a fleet of more than 120 privateers to be fitted out in New York, with the goal of preying on the shipments of the enemy. Thus, work was created for thousands of seamen, and privateering attracted "immense quantities of goods and money into the local economy." In a six-month period between September 1778 and March 1779, more than 165 prizes were brought into New York. Their value was approximately £600,000. Once again, "shopkeepers, cloakmakers, milliners, dressmakers, wigmakers, and coachmakers" attempted to meet the demand of the local population, especially the military officers' and privateers' wives and children. Additionally, merchants made a ton of money through illicit trade with the Patriot-held areas of New Jersey and Connecticut, despite the fact that authorities on both sides tried to put a stop to it. In 1782, Alexander Hamilton estimated that Patriots in upstate New York bought more than

£30,000 worth of luxury items from New York City merchants annually. And each year, they bought over £80,000 worth of luxury goods from New Jersey, Pennsylvania and New England. There was so much currency entering New York City every week that Loyalist merchants were making enormous profits.[204]

One of the "great crucibles" of the American Revolution focused on the 150 miles of coastline between New York Bay and Delaware Bay, the "very portals to the two power centers of war, Philadelphia and New York."[205] And for the fledgling American government to engage in a naval conflict with Great Britain was like "an infant taking a mad bull by his horns." It would, many argued, "ruin the character and corrupt the morals of our seamen… [making] them selfish, piratical, mercenary, bent wholly on plunder."[206] Colonial leaders debated the merits and pitfalls of constructing an American fleet and how they might mount some defense at sea against the British. Despite opposition to the scheme, Congress appointed a committee to prepare an expense estimate and to develop a proposal for the creation of a Continental navy. It was obvious, however, that a Continental fleet could never equal the Royal Navy, especially in such a short period. Silas Deane of Connecticut and others "firmly believed that to adequately contest the enemy on the high seas and injure him where it most hurt, namely in his overseas commerce, it would be necessary to also authorize the fielding of private vessels of war, which could be accomplished at private expense, with little economic burden to the public." And why not? Privateers had been incredibly important in the previous conflicts with the French and had made many merchants and mariners extremely wealthy. Yet Deane was keenly aware of the dangers in this proposal—unleashing privateers without proper measures of control and administration. Deane argued that it was a "justifiable piracy" but that there was no doubt that "the consequences may be very pernicious" if these measures of control were not implemented.[207]

The day before the *Asia* arrived in the East River and tested the loyalties of New York residents, another warship rounded Cape Henlopen and set a course for Lewes Harbor in the Delaware Bay. Months before, a Delaware Bay pilot named Henry Fisher had been instructed by the revolutionary government of Philadelphia to report on any warships that entered Delaware Bay. As the war spread, it was clear that the Royal Navy intended to take control of the bay. Fisher knew all too well that they didn't have the necessary ships to take on the Royal Navy, members of which Fisher referred to as pirates. Fisher had a keen knowledge of the bay and its shoals. So, to prevent the Royal Navy from sailing into the bay, he ordered all the buoys

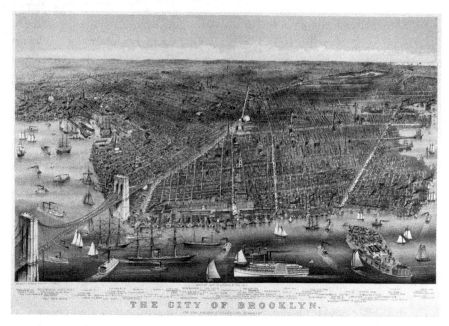

The City of Brooklyn, by Currier and Ives, 1879. *Image from Wikimedia Commons.*

that marked the shoals be removed. He also instituted a series of alarms to warn the locals of British arrivals. First, if a British ship entered the bay, lanterns set up at the Cape Henlopen Lighthouse would be lit, and guns would be fired. Second, he set up a system by which news of British warships and their movements could quickly travel up the coast to Philadelphia.[208]

These preventative measures proved useful, as there was little activity in or near the bay for many months—that is, until an American squadron comprising eight warships under the command of Commodore Esek Hopkins arrived in February 1776. Hopkins referred to his squadron as the First Continental Fleet. They remained in the bay for several days before heading to the Bahamas, where they hoped to disrupt materiel transfers for the British.[209] But their presence alone had done much to increase morale among the local Patriots. That all changed on March 25, 1776, when a British squadron arrived, led by the frigate *Roebuck*. The *Roebuck* was commanded by a Captain Andrew Snape Hamond. Despite Fisher's carefully laid warning system, a series of missteps prevented his warnings from reaching the messengers to relay up the coast. So Fisher took it upon himself to send a note to the colonial authorities in Philadelphia, warning them that a squadron had entered the bay, and he promised that they would do all they could to not allow any pilots or ships from being impressed into British service.[210] As Fisher's messenger rode up the coast to Philadelphia, Captain Hamond and his men seized a boat they believed to be a messenger ship.

News of the British squadron's arrival traveled throughout the local area quite quickly, and more than one thousand militiamen assembled to defend Lewes and the bay from the enemy. In the meantime, Captain Hamond was having no luck in finding a pilot to impress into service. Unaware of the many shallows in the bay, Captain Hamond ran the *Roebuck* aground several times. The British did manage to seize a few merchant ships, but the local pilots realized they could avoid the British by simply keeping close to shore. On April 7, 1776, Captain Hamond saw a small schooner rounding Cape Henlopen. The schooner was commanded by a Lewes local named Captain Nehemiah Field. Aware that the British were lurking in the bay, Captain Field steered his schooner close to the shore. Captain Hamond responded by sending out several small boats to seize the goods aboard the schooner, as well as their pilot, Captain Field. But as the schooner neared the shore, a company of Continental soldiers arrived and marched toward the schooner. The British, unwilling to lose this prize, began firing at the schooner and the Continental soldiers. But the soldiers held their ground, unloading the schooner. It was observed that "a hot fire from both sides ensued, which lasted nearly two hours," after which the British sulked in defeat. Overall, Fisher's efforts to prevent the British from seizing local pilots or boats was successful. And for the rest of the American Revolution, the British would have difficulty in the Delaware Bay without pilots to guide them through the shallows.[211]

LET'S MAKE IT OFFICIAL

B y April 1776, Congress was ready to take the plunge into the realm of privateering. The authorization signed by John Jay stated that the privateers "may, by force of arms, attack, subdue, and take all ships and other vessels belonging to the subjects of the king of Great Britain," as well as "all ships and other vessels whatsoever carrying soldiers arms, gun-powder, ammunition, provisions, or any other contraband goods, to any of the British armies or ships of war employed against these colonies." After the seizure of any such ship, the privateer was to bring the vessel to the nearest port to await a court trial to be judged. They were not to, "in cold blood, kill or maim, or by torture or otherwise, cruelly, inhumanly, and contrary to common usage and the practice of civilized nations in war" any prisoner of war they took.[212] One such letter of marque was issued by the Continental Congress, signed by John Hancock, in October 1776. The commission was issued to James Powell, commander of the three-ton schooner *Northampton*.[213] In all, more than seven hundred letters of marque were granted by the Continental Congress. And one of the most important home ports for vessels operating as privateers was the dock at Philadelphia. The British immediately retaliated and passed the Treason Act in 1777. It made American privateering an illegal action (or piracy) supported by an illegitimate congress. In the meantime, the British provided commissions to approximately eight hundred of their own privateers.[214]

Perhaps one of the most audacious privateers of the American Revolution was William Treen of Pennsylvania. He got his start as a crew member on

The Sages and Heroes of the American Revolution, Including the Signers of the Declaration of Independence (Portrait of John Manly), by Levi Carroll Judson, 1854. *Image from Wikimedia Commons.*

board the *Hawk*, commanded by Enoch Stillwell. It was granted its letter of marque in September 1779 and immediately set sail to ravage the British. The *Hawk* was a schooner mounted with approximately ten cannons and 80 men, including the intrepid Treen. But the *Hawk* was to have a very short-lived career as a privateer, and many of its men would perish. It was spotted just a few days after setting sail by a pair of British frigates, one of them being the *Galatea*, a sixth-rate ship with approximately twenty guns and 140 men, captained by Thomas Jordan.[215] As Stillwell and his crew tried to escape the frigates, they were cut off. One of the frigates sailed straight for the *Hawk* with the intention of ramming the tiny schooner. Fearing for their lives, many of the men jumped ship, while others braced themselves for impact. The contact between the two ships nearly ripped the *Hawk* in half, and much of the remaining crew fell into the water.[216]

Treen managed to make it on board the *Galatea*, but his fellow crew members weren't so fortunate. It was reported that the British chopped at the hands and arms of those trying to climb aboard. Treen demanded that the British stop their barbarity, but they refused and allowed seventy-eight men to perish. Rather than execute Treen, however, the British were impressed by his courage and instead imprisoned him on board a dreaded prison ship called the *Jersey*, which was anchored in New York Harbor. Treen's heroic actions landed him a fair number of Patriot supporters along the shore of New Jersey. But life aboard the *Jersey* was nothing short of hell. It was a filthy, rat-infested disease factory. It's unclear how long Treen managed to survive on board the *Jersey*, but he made a daring escape before the beginning of 1780. He was lauded as a hero by locals, and his exploits were printed in Patriot broadsheets in New York, Philadelphia and beyond. And he was mentioned in every major newspaper.[217]

Treen decided to take his newfound celebrity and use it to his advantage. He convinced Joseph Carson, a prominent merchant and well-known backer of Patriot privateers, to finance a venture. In March 1780, Treen was offered command of the *Rattlesnake*, a forty-ton schooner. Treen armed the vessel with six two-pounder guns and six swivel guns and gathered a crew of approximately thirty-five men. The crew was met with immediate success. On March 22, 1780, they captured their first prize: a Loyalist trading sloop called the *Hazard*, which had once been an American privateer.[218] Treen and his men took the *Hazard* to the nearest port and reaped the benefits of the sale of its valuable cargo, including sugar, rum, coffee and molasses. The cargo was auctioned off at a public venue on March 30, 1780.[219] Treen and his men went back to the sea as soon as they refitted their ship. In April 1780, Treen and his men took another trading sloop, the *Speedwell*, which was actually an American ship that had been seized by the British and renamed the *Dispatch*. Its goods, tackle, apparel and furniture were to be sold on May 4 at a public venue in Little Egg Harbor.[220]

Summer was relatively slow for the men of the *Rattlesnake*, although they seized a schooner called the *Betsey* in June. They also took two schooners in October, the *Flying Fish* and the *Saturday-Night*. Treen's investors were pleased with his performance, as was Congress. As a reward for his success, his investors offered him a much larger ship, a square-rigged brig called *Fame*, which Treen had taken as a prize in December 1780. The *Fame* had ten cannons for his use. How would Treen do with a larger ship at his disposal? In just a few short weeks, he found out when he seized the British privateer the *Cock*, which was headed from New York to the Chesapeake Bay.[221] High off the capture of his latest vessel, Treen decided to anchor near the mouth of Egg Harbor. While there, he resupplied and refit the ship before heading back out on his mission. But fate was not on his side on that bitterly cold January day. On January 22, 1781, Treen and a couple of his men were on shore, buying the necessary supplies to refit the ship, while the rest of the crew remained aboard to guard the vessel against Loyalist privateers. At flood tide, the *Fame* capsized, throwing its crewmen into the frigid waters. Some of the men clung desperately to the rough planking of the overturned ship. Four others, Thomas Adams, Eleazer Crawford, Jacob Corson and a man known as Steelman, loosened one of the lifeboats and managed to make it to shore—all except Steelman, that is, who was washed away by a breaker as they were nearing the beach.[222]

There were four others who managed to survive, having clung to the utterly destroyed hull of the ship. They were rescued the following morning by Treen and a group of volunteers. A total of twenty-five men died as a result of this accident.[223] But Treen hadn't given up privateering just yet. By the summer of 1781, he was co-captaining a whaleboat called the *Unity* along with Joseph Edwards. Treen's last recorded capture occurred on January 3, 1782. He came across a schooner that was coming out of Jones Creek, which was a well-known spot for Loyalist smugglers. So Treen and his crew decided to seize the vessel, believing it to be well loaded with profitable goods. It turned out to be the *Betsey*, which Treen had captured just a year and a half earlier. Treen learned that the *Betsey* had been sold to an American merchant before it was captured by the British and sold to a Loyalist smuggler. Treen tried to place the ship up for auction, but its former owner (the Patriot merchant) sued to have the ship returned to him as its rightful owner. Little is known of Treen after this affair.

Treen wasn't the only privateer to patrol the waters between Delaware and New York. Privateers on the Delaware Bay were integral to the success of the Americans during the American Revolution. And those in Cape May were some of the most important. They were made up of local boys, as well as merchants, mariners and militiamen from Cumberland County to the northwest and Gloucester County, New Jersey (which is now Atlantic County). The Cape May Peninsula is strategically located between Philadelphia and New York. It is surrounded on three sides by water and sits between the Atlantic Ocean and the Delaware Bay. There were only about two thousand people living in Cape May County in 1775, but most of the men were either full- or part-time mariners. They were ship captains, crewmen or pilots. What's important is that they were intimately familiar with the intricacies of the "ever-changing contours of the inlets, bays, channels, and sandbars—knowledge that would serve them well when trying to avoid any British or refugee (Tory) vessels that outgunned them."[224] Much like other privateers throughout the nation, the Cape May privateers were financed by merchant investors who put up the necessary capital to purchase and outfit the vessels.

While Cape May's residents were more than happy to attack British shipping and disrupt Royal Navy vessels, the same could not be said of their northerly neighbors in Burlington County or Monmouth County. Patriots often had to fear the strength of the British forces and the Loyalists among them.[225]

Being captured by the British was often tortuous, as seen in the experience of Treen. We also get a glimpse of life on board a prison ship from John Ingersoll of New Jersey, who was captured and spent two months on a prison ship/makeshift hospital, the *Huntress*. Ingersoll recounted how he was transferred from the prison ship the *Scorpion* after he was "taken sick with a camp fever." But Ingersoll found no relief. He was soon "attacked" with dysentery. He hoped that this would actually bring an end to his suffering, but although "death relieved some of my messmates from the horrors of that prison," Ingersoll was among those who recovered. As far as provisions went, the prisoners were provided a half pound of mutton a day, but the "mutton" was really just the heads of the sheep with the horns and wool still attached.[226] The prisoners made the best of a horrible situation by taking their "bread," which was just oatmeal that had not been sifted, and pounding "up a sheep's head until the bones were all broken," creating something of a stew.[227] In many cases, American privateers who were captured by the British were not considered prisoners of war. Instead, they were accused of rebellion, treason and piracy, in which case, the British suspended habeas corpus and deemed the privateers ineligible for prisoner exchange.

11

DETRACTORS, BLACK SAILORS
AND THE CONCLUSION OF WAR

The American privateers devastated British shipping and maritime commerce during the war. Privateering also drove up maritime insurance rates and the cost of imported goods. According to the British House of Lords, for example, an astonishing 559 vessels had been taken by American privateers by February 1778. During the course of the war, the Continental navy seized somewhere between 100 and 200 English prizes, while mid-Atlantic privateers brought in an impressive 600-plus ships. Conservative estimates of the total number of ships seized by all privateers is approximately 2,300. To get a sense of just how big a menace American privateers were, there were 270 British warships at the beginning of the American Revolution and more than 470 by the end of the war in 1783—a substantial but necessary increase to combat the Patriot privateers. Not all Patriots were impressed by the actions of the American privateers, however. A Continental naval officer named John Paul Jones observed that "the common classes of mankind are actuated by no noble principle [other] than that of self-interest. This and only this determines all adventurers in privateers, the owners as well as those whom they employ."[228] And despite his investment in a privateering venture, General Henry Knox's wife, Lucy Knox, wrote to him that she did "not like privateering" and that, often, property is taken from "innocent persons, who have nothing to do with the quarrel—[it] appears to me to be very unjust."[229]

Privateering during the American Revolution also had an impact on both enslaved and free Black men. Unlike the Continental army, the navy was more than willing to recruit both free and enslaved Black men, due to a

Gosport, Flagship Saluting, by Edward William Cooke, circa 1777. *Courtesy of the New York Public Library.*

lack of available sailors. Many Black men along the coasts were experienced sailors and mariners, which made them valuable members of any crew. For many Black men, privateering seemed much more appealing than serving in the Continental navy. According to some estimates, Black men made up approximately 10 percent of a typical American privateer's crew. One example is the crew of the *Fair American,* one of the more successful privateers sailing out of New York, which was recorded as having at least four Black men among its crew: Cato Ramsey, Daniel Fisher, Luke Wilson and June. For the enslaved who escaped, there was less chance of being caught by slave catchers if they became privateers, spending much of their time off shore. And there was a greater financial reward in privateering, since the owners/investors and the crewmen equally divided the spoils. The state and federal governments did not get a share, although the Continental navy's prizes were divided down the middle between the Continental Congress and the crew members. Congress's share was later reduced to one-third in order to encourage more prize-taking.[230] But many enslaved Black men found themselves victims of a scheme called a substitution system, in which they served in their owner's place, while their owners received their pay. For example, in 1780, William Smith, a Woodbridge Loyalist, sent an enslaved Black man named Andrew out on a New York privateer in the hopes that he would profit from Andrew's maritime service. But the New York privateer that Andrew served on was captured. So not only did Smith lose Andrew, but he also failed to earn any prize money. It is unclear what happened to Andrew, although it is safe to assume that he was sold back into slavery somewhere in the American colonies. Additionally, although the British offered freedom to any Black man who served in the Royal Navy or joined a British privateering vessel, particularly on the waterfront of New York, Black mariners who served on captured British ships typically found themselves sold back into slavery. For example, a Black sailor named Patrick Dennis was on a captured privateering vessel and brought to Philadelphia, where he was sold back into slavery. Dennis was one of the fortunate few who escaped and returned to privateering as a means of maintaining his freedom.[231]

Perhaps the most famous of these Black sailors was a free Black man named James Forten, who enlisted as a powder boy at the tender age of fourteen on the privateer *Royal Louis*, commanded by Captain Stephen Decatur Sr. Unfortunately, the *Royal Louis* was captured by a British warship commanded by Captain John Bazely, and Forten was taken prisoner, along with the rest of the crew. Bazely was, according to accounts, impressed with Forten and treated him as a prisoner of war rather than a pirate, contrary to British law. Forten was transferred to HMS *Jersey*, where he languished for seven miserable months in the disease-infested ship until he was released in a prisoner exchange.[232] Forten would later become a famous abolitionist and reformer.

As the American Revolution came to an end in 1783, the need for privateers also came to an end—albeit briefly. In all, the American privateers contributed significantly to the war effort, devastating British shipping to the tune of about $18 million by the end of the war. Following the war, many privateers turned to serving as captains or crew members aboard merchant ships, while many others wondered what was next for them. Benjamin Franklin tried, unsuccessfully, to include an article banning privateering in future wars in the Treaty of Paris. In the postwar years, the government found that it was expensive to maintain a standing navy. While president, Thomas Jefferson severely cut the size and resources of the United States Navy. But in just a couple of decades, the United States found itself again in need of privateers, as a number of international incidents hinted at a war to come. When the War of 1812 broke out, the United States relied heavily on its privateers, keeping its navy relatively small, as a means of preventing a full-scale naval war with Britain. In all, the government commissioned approximately 525 private ships as privateers, and they captured thousands of British vessels and millions of dollars' worth of prizes.

PART III

I AM THE SEA AND NOBODY OWNS ME

Do you fear death? Do you fear that dark abyss? All your deeds laid bare. All your sins punished. I can offer you...an escape.

—*Davy Jones,* Pirates of the Caribbean

12

I AM THE INNOCENTEST PERSON OF THEM ALL

For decades, pirates were not only incredibly successful in lining their own pockets but also useful tools in the process of colonialism in the Atlantic world. Pirates supplemented the incomes of burgeoning colonies, helping them grow and stabilize. They not only brought the goods and resources that colonists wanted and needed but helped forcibly transport enslaved Africans to the colonies, which fueled colonial expansion and made many colonists very wealthy. In many ways, the colonies needed the pirates as much as the pirates needed the colonies. Despite their "stateless" nature, pirates couldn't have operated without colonial support. It was through this support that they were able to fence their loot, refit and resupply their ships and find willing crew members to serve. This support also saved many of their lives. For example, we can look to the case of the aforementioned Moses Butterworth, who, in 1701, found himself imprisoned in Middletown, New Jersey, after confessing to serving with Captain Kidd. It was the support of a local leader named Samuel Willet that secured Butterworth's freedom. Willet gathered together a group of men, and armed with guns and clubs, they made their way to the courthouse, where Butterworth was being questioned. Some estimated that the crowd of angry East Jersey residents numbered at least one hundred. During the chaos, locals Benjamin and Richard Borden (who were injured in the scuffle) successfully released Butterworth and, in turn, took Governor Hamilton, his supporters and the sheriff as their prisoners. The open and explicit support of piracy was a prominent feature of the mid-Atlantic colonies, especially in New York and Philadelphia. But the support could not last forever, and the tides began to turn against the pirates in the 1710s. For all their attempts to fight the Crown's increasing regulations of things, like the appointment of governors, the structure of their courts and their restrictive economic policies, the colonists began to recognize the long-term benefits of legal trade, especially as commercial opportunities expanded and the barbaric trade in enslaved people flourished, which created a new social order in the colonies. No longer were the colonists benefiting from piracy; instead, their economic security was increasingly threatened by the pirates, who began attacking British and American vessels.[233] With increased cooperation from imperial authorities and the changing attitudes of colonists in America and the Caribbean, piracy decreased dramatically. Despite frequent protestations of innocence, more pirates were executed in this brief period than they had been in earlier decades.

But the spirit of piracy was not entirely eradicated. When war broke out between the American colonists seeking independence and Great Britain, both nations turned to privateers to supplement their naval forces and to disrupt each other's commerce. The American implementation of privateering was met with great success. Thousands of British ships were captured, damaged or destroyed over the course of the war. And American privateers caused millions of dollars' worth of damage to British commerce. While their actions were considered patriotic, contributing to the American war effort, not all privateers were motivated by love of country or support of the Revolution. Indeed, many, it seems, were motivated more by the promise of personal gain, as privateers could earn significantly more in prize money than the average Continental navy sailor could earn from their salary. As a result, there was a swelling in the ranks of privateers, while the Continental navy struggled to obtain and keep recruits. We see the impact of privateering most dramatically, perhaps, in the mid-Atlantic where the 150 miles of coastline between New York Bay and Delaware Bay, home to the major power centers of New York and Philadelphia, were hotly contested. The mid-Atlantic, especially New York and Philadelphia, benefited significantly from the presence and support of privateers, whether they were American or British. Although they were operating with legal permission from their respective governments, in the eyes of many, enemy privateers were no better than the pirates of the previous decades. Despite some reservations about the use of American privateers from men like John Paul Jones and Benjamin Franklin, they were ultimately deemed a necessary component of the American war machine. Privateering would further prove to be beneficial for the new nation during the subsequent War of 1812 and for the Confederates during the American Civil War.

From Captain Kidd, who declared himself the "innocentest person of them all," to the anonymous pirate who admitted that he repented only that he "had not done more mischief," that he and his fellow pirates "did not cut the throats of them that took us" and that he was "extremely sorry that you aren't hanged as well as we," pirates ran the gamut from unlikely contributors to the Atlantic World economy to violent usurpers of authority and detriments to economic stability.[234] This was readily apparent in the mid-Atlantic colonies, which benefited greatly from trade and association with pirates in the late seventeenth and early eighteenth centuries. As the need for piracy turned to the need for privateers, the mid-Atlantic continued to prove the deep connection it had with sea marauders, serving as home to some of the most successful and prolific of both American and British privateers. Without the influence and impact of both pirates and privateers, the development of the mid-Atlantic might have looked very different.

NOTES

Chapter 1

1. A foremast man is a man stationed to attend to the gear of the foremast, a common sailor.
2. "Coast of Crocus" may refer to Crocus Bay in Anguilla, one of the most northerly of the Leeward Islands in the Lesser Antilles. Anguilla is east of Puerto Rico and the Virgin Islands and lies directly north of St. Martin.
3. "The Case of Samuell Burgess," SP 34/36, f. 35.
4. Ibid.
5. Ibid.
6. "Gulph of Mocca" refers to the Gulph of Mocha, also known as al-Makha. It is a port city on the Red Sea coast of Yemen.
7. "Examinations of John Brown &c.," *Trials of Eight Persons*, 23–25.
8. "America and West Indies: December 1718, 11–19: 797. Governor Hamilton to the Council of Trade and Plantations," *Calendar of State Papers Colonial*, 30:404–24.
9. "America and West Indies: December 1718, 11–19: 797. vi. Deposition of Robert Leonard, Commander of the snow *Eagle* of New York," *Calendar of State Papers Colonial*, 30:404–24.
10. Kyriakodis, *Lost Waterfront*, 103–4.
11. "America and West Indies: September 1699, 1–15: 769. xviii. Lord Bellomont to Lords of the Admiralty, Boston, Sept. 7, '99," *Calendar of State Papers Colonial*, 17:420–39.
12. Lydon, *Pirates*, 25–26.
13. Ritchie, *Captain Kidd*, 33.
14. Ibid.

15. "America and West Indies: January 1699, 16–31: 51. Reasons Why the Revenue of New York was Not So Great 1692–1697 as in 1687," *Calendar of State Papers Colonial*, 17:19–34.
16. Ritchie, *Captain Kidd*, 34.
17. Ibid., 35.
18. Ibid.
19. Rogoziński, *Honor Among Thieves*, 111.
20. A series of contractual relationships between the upper classes, designed to maintain control over land.
21. Rogoziński, *Honor Among Thieves*, 111–12.
22. "Weaver's Reply," CO 391/11, f. 215–16; Ritchie, *Captain Kidd*, 38; "America and West Indies: January 1699, 1–14: 8. Deposition of Capt. John Evans, Late Commander of H.M. Frigate *Richmond*," *Calendar of State Papers Colonial*, 1–19; Burrows and Wallace, *Gotham*, 17:106.
23. "America and West Indies: November 1698, 21–25: 1,007. Heads of Charges Relating to Governor Fletcher's Administration at New York, Delivered to Him at the Board, 28 November 1698," *Calendar of State Papers Colonial*, 16:560–64.
24. "America and West Indies: January 1699, 1–14: 26. T. Weaver to the Council of Trade and Plantations," *Calendar of State Papers Colonial*, 17:1–19.
25. Burrows and Wallace, *Gotham*, 106.
26. Rediker, *Between the Devil*, 72.
27. Burrows and Wallace, *Gotham*, 106.
28. "America and West Indies: May 1698, 16–20: 475. Journal of the House of Representatives of New York," *Calendar of State Papers Colonial*, 16:217–34.
29. Ritchie, *Captain Kidd*, 36–37.
30. Hanna, *Pirate Nests*, 235.
31. Ibid., 235.
32. Fox, *Pirates*, 307.
33. Ritchie, *Captain Kidd*, 37.
34. "Deposition of Adam Baldridge, 5 May 1699," CO 5/1042, no. 30ii.
35. "America and West Indies: May 1717, 16–31: 595. i. Information of Andrew Turbett, Master, and Robert Gilmor, Supercargo of the *Agnis* of Glasgow, 17th April 1717," *Calendar of State Papers Colonial*, 29:303–22.
36. "A List of the Prices that Capt. Jacobs Sold Licquors and Other Goods att St. Mary's, 9 June 1698," HCA 1/98, f. 142.
37. "Deposition of Adam Baldridge, 5 May 1699," CO 5/1042, no. 30ii.
38. "America and West Indies: March 1700, 1–10: 190. Robert Quary to the Commissioners of Customs," *Calendar of State Papers Colonial*, 18:99–115.
39. "America and West Indies: June 1698, 21–25: 593. Governor the Earl of Bellomont to Council of Trade and Plantations," *Calendar of State Papers Colonial*, 16:278–91.
40. "America and West Indies: May 1698, 16–20: 472. Governor the Earl of Bellomont to Council of Trade and Plantations," *Calendar of State Papers Colonial*, 16:217–34.

41. "America and West Indies: November 1698, 21–25: 1,007. Heads of Charges Relating to Governor Fletcher's Administration at New York, Delivered to Him at the Board, 28 November 1698," *Calendar of State Papers Colonial*, 16:560–64.

42. "America and West Indies: June 1698, 21–25: 593. Governor the Earl of Bellomont to Council of Trade and Plantations," *Calendar of State Papers Colonial*, 16:278–91.

43. "America and West Indies: June 1698, 21–25: 593. viii. Deposition of John Pantree. 8 June 1698," *Calendar of State Papers Colonial*, 16:278–91.

44. "America and West Indies: May 1699, 11–15: 384. Governor the Earl of Bellomont to the Council of Trade and Plantations," *Calendar of State Papers Colonial*, 17:208–24.

45. "America and West Indies: May 1698, 16–20: 473. Governor the Earl of Bellomont to Council of Trade and Plantations," *Calendar of State Papers Colonial*, 16:217–34.

46. "America and West Indies: May 1698, 16–20: 473. iii. Deposition of Edward Taylor. 7 May 1698," *Calendar of State Papers Colonial*, 16:217–34; "America and West Indies: October 1698, 17–20: 904. Council of Trade and Plantations to the Lords Justices of England," *Calendar of State Papers Colonial*, 16:478–85.

47. "America and West Indies: June 1698, 21–25: 593. Governor the Earl of Bellomont to Council of Trade and Plantations," *Calendar of State Papers Colonial*, 16:278–91.

48. "America and West Indies: May 1698, 16–20: 472. Governor the Earl of Bellomont to Council of Trade and Plantations," *Calendar of State Papers Colonial*, 16:217–34.

49. "America and West Indies: February 1698, 1–15: 224. Narrative of Mr. Henry Watson, who was Taken 'Prisoner by the Pirates,' 15 August 1696," *Calendar of State Papers Colonial*, 16:97–111.

50. "America and West Indies: August 1698, 22–25: 770. Information of Henry Watson," *Calendar of State Papers Colonial*, 16:399–406.

51. "America and West Indies: May 1699, 11–15: 384. Governor the Earl of Bellomont to the Council of Trade and Plantations," *Calendar of State Papers Colonial*, 17:208–24.

52. "America and West Indies: August 1699, 7–10: 706. Council of Trade and Plantations to the Lords Justices," *Calendar of State Papers Colonial*, 17:385–88.

53. "America and West Indies: June 1698, 21–25: 593. Governor the Earl of Bellomont to Council of Trade and Plantations," *Calendar of State Papers Colonial*, 16:278–91.

54. "America and West Indies: August 1699, 7–10: 706. Council of Trade and Plantations to the Lords Justices," *Calendar of State Papers Colonial*, 17:385–88.

55. Ibid.

56. "America and West Indies: July 1699, 21–25: 675. Governor the Earl of Bellomont to the Council of Trade and Plantations," *Calendar of State Papers Colonial*, 17:357–66.

57. "America and West Indies: January 1701, 1–3: 7. Governor the Earl of Bellomont to Mr. Secretary Vernon," *Calendar of State Papers Colonial*, 19:1–17.
58. "America and West Indies: July 1699, 6–10: 621. Governor Lord Bellomont to the Council of Trade and Plantations," *Calendar of State Papers Colonial*, 17:327–40.
59. "America and West Indies: March 1699, 1–10: 169. Memorial From Several Merchants Trading to New York to the Council of Trade and Plantations," *Calendar of State Papers Colonial*, 17:82–101.
60. "America and West Indies: February 1699, 1–4: 66. Council of Trade and Plantations to the Earl of Bellomont," *Calendar of State Papers Colonial*, 17:34–51.
61. "Letter of Lord Bellomont," *Calendar of Treasury Papers*, 172–83.

Chapter 2

62. "America and West Indies: August 1696, 17–31: 149. I. A Paper Submitted to the Commissioners of Customs by Edward Randolph. 17 Aug. 1696," *Calendar of State Papers Colonial*, 15:71–91.
63. "America and West Indies: October 1699, 16–20: 877. Col. Quary to the Council of Trade and Plantations," *Calendar of State Papers Colonial*, 17:463–82.
64. "America and West Indies: August 1698, 16–20: Robert Quarry to Governor Nicholson. Philadelphia, 6 August 1698," *Calendar of State Papers Colonial*, 16:377–99.
65. Quoted in Hanna, *Pirate Nests*, 280.
66. "America and West Indies: September 1698, 6–10: 796. Robert Quarry to Council of Trade and Plantations," *Calendar of State Papers Colonial*, 16:413–20.
67. "America and West Indies: August 1698, 16–20: 759. i. Address of the General Assembly of Pennsylvania to the King," *Calendar of State Papers Colonial*, 16:377–99.
68. Ibid.
69. "America and West Indies: September 1697, 17–30: 1,331. Robert Snead to Sir John Houblon," *Calendar of State Papers Colonial*, 15:611–26.
70. Ibid.
71. "America and West Indies: April 1698, 18–30: 403. Robert Snead to Sir John Houblon," *Calendar of State Papers Colonial*, 16:171–87.
72. "America and West Indies: October 1699, 16–20: Copy of Deposition of Jacob Bodill, Ship's Carpenter, James Hunt and Harman Peterson, Newcastle, July 27, 1699," *Calendar of State Papers Colonial*, 17:463–82.
73. "America and West Indies: October 1699, 16–20: (6) Copy of Letter of Math. Birche," *Calendar of State Papers Colonial*, 17:463–82.
74. "America and West Indies: October 1699, 16–20: 878. Governor the Earl of Bellomont to the Council of Trade and Plantations," *Calendar of State Papers Colonial*, 17:463–82.
75. "America and West Indies: October 1699, 16–20: 877. i. (1) Petition of Inhabitants of Newcastle to Governor Markham," *Calendar of State Papers Colonial*, 17:463–82.
76. Morgan, *Pirates & Patriots*, 14.

77. Ritchie, *Captain Kidd*, 37.
78. "America and West Indies: October 1698, 17–20: 904. Council of Trade and Plantations to the Lords Justices of England," *Calendar of State Papers Colonial*, 16:478–85.
79. Ritchie, *Captain Kidd*, 38; Hanna, *Pirate Nests*, 219.
80. "America and West Indies: June 1698, 21–25: 593. xvii. Deposition of John Wick. 2 June 1698," *Calendar of State Papers Colonial*, 16:278–91.
81. "America and West Indies: May 1698, 16–20: 473. Governor the Earl of Bellomont to Council of Trade and Plantations," *Calendar of State Papers Colonial*, 16:217–34.
82. He was also known as Robert Glover.
83. "America and West Indies: December 1697, 16–31: 115. i. Copies of Extracts from Letters Received by the East India Company," *Calendar of State Papers Colonial*, 16:61–78.
84. Lydon, *Pirates*, 43.
85. "America and West Indies: December 1697, 16–31: From Captain Thomas Warren, of H.M.S. *Windsor*, to the East India Company, 28 November 1697," *Calendar of State Papers Colonial*, 16:61–78.
86. Hanna, *Pirate Nests*, 169–70.
87. Quoted in Hanna, *Pirate Nests*, 219.
88. Hanna, *Pirate Nests*, 170–71.
89. Quoted in Hanna, *Pirate Nests*, 221.
90. Rediker, *Between the Devil*, 256.
91. Quoted in Hanna, *Pirate Nests*, 5.
92. "Penn to BOT, Philadelphia, April 28, 1700," CO 5/1260, no. 43.
93. Quoted in Hanna, *Pirate Nests*, 215.
94. Hanna, *Pirate Nests*, 12.
95. Ibid., 5.
96. Ibid.
97. Ibid., 10.
98. Also known as the Spanish Dollar, pieces of eight were silver coins, approximately thirty-eight millimeters (one and a half inches) in diameter, worth eight Spanish reales (Judd, "Frederick Philipse," 354–74).
99. "The Examination of Richard Roper, 27 August 1701," HCA 1.53, ff. 100–101.
100. "America and West Indies: January 1719: 31, i, Mr. Gale to Col. Thomas Pitt, Junr. So. Carolina, 4th Nov. 1718," *Calendar of State Papers Colonial*, 31:1–21.
101. Hanna, *Pirate Nests*, 7.
102. Ibid., 14.
103. Quoted in Hanna, *Pirate Nests*, 178.
104. "America and West Indies: January 1701, 1–3: 3. Governor the Earl of Bellomont to the Council of Trade and Plantations," *Calendar of State Papers Colonial*, 19:1–17.
105. "America and West Indies: May 1698, 16–20: 473. Governor the Earl of Bellomont to Council of Trade and Plantations," *Calendar of State Papers Colonial*,

16:217–34; "America and West Indies: January 1699, 1–14: 26. T. Weaver to the Council of Trade and Plantations," *Calendar of State Papers Colonial*, 17:1–19.

106. "America and West Indies: July 1698, 6–9: 647. Governor Goddard to the Duke of Shrewsbury," *Calendar of State Papers Colonial*, 16:322–28.

107. Lydon, *Pirates*, 38–39.

Chapter 3

108. "America and West Indies: July 1697, 12–20: 1,187. Jeremiah Basse to William Popple," *Calendar of State Papers Colonial*, 15:545–60.

109. Hanna, *Pirate Nests*, 263.

110. Ibid., 263–65.

111. "America and West Indies: July 1697, 21–31: 1,198. William Popple to Jeremiah Basse," *Calendar of State Papers Colonial*, 15:560–71.

112. "America and West Indies: July 1697, 21–31: 1,203. Jeremiah Basse to William Popple," *Calendar of State Papers Colonial*, 15:560–71.

113. Ibid.

114. Ibid.

115. Ibid.

116. "America and West Indies: December 1700, 6–10: 983. Governor the Earl of Bellomont to Mr. Secretary Vernon," *Calendar of State Papers Colonial*, 18:716–31.

117. Hanna, *Pirate Nests*, 267–68.

118. "America and West Indies: April 1698, 18–30: 415. Governor Basse to William Popple," *Calendar of State Papers Colonial*, 16:171–87.

119. "America and West Indies: November 1697, 27–29: 76. i. Robert Quarry to William Penn. London [*blanks for dates unfilled*], 1697," *Calendar of State Papers Colonial*, 16:37–53.

120. "America and West Indies: November 1697, 27–29: 76. xii. Governor Markham to William Penn. 13 Feb. 1696–7," *Calendar of State Papers Colonial*, 16:37–53.

121. "America and West Indies: November 1697, 27–29: 76. i. Robert Quarry to William Penn. London [*blanks for dates unfilled*], 1697," *Calendar of State Papers Colonial*, 16:37–53.

122. "America and West Indies: November 1697, 27–29: 76. vii. Captain Josiah Daniell to Governor Markham," *Calendar of State Papers Colonial*, 16:37–53.

123. "America and West Indies: November 1697, 27–29: 76. viii. Governor Markham to Captain Daniell. Philadelphia, 30 March 1697," *Calendar of State Papers Colonial*, 16:37–53.

124. "America and West Indies: May 1698, 11–14: 451. Edward Randolph to William Popple," *Calendar of State Papers Colonial*, 16:207–17.

125. "America and West Indies: April 1698, 18–30: 401. Edward Randolph to William Popple," *Calendar of State Papers Colonial*, 16:171–87.

126. "America and West Indies: March 1700, 1–10: 176. Col. Markham to the Council of Trade and Plantations," *Calendar of State Papers Colonial*, 18:99–115.

127. Hanna, *Pirate Nests*, 288–89.

128. Ibid., 270–71.

129. "America and West Indies: May 1700, 21–25: 466. Governor the Earl of Bellomont to the Council of Trade and Plantations," *Calendar of State Papers Colonial*, 18:263–84.

Chapter 4

130. "America and West Indies: May 1698, 16–20: 473. vii. Deposition of Leonard Lewis," *Calendar of State Papers Colonial*, 16:217–34.

131. "America and West Indies: May 1698, 6–10: 433. Minutes of Council of New York," *Calendar of State Papers Colonial*, 16:191–206.

132. "America and West Indies: September 1698, 21–25: 835. iv. Copy of a Letter from Governor Markham to Governor Lord Bellomont. Philadelphia, 31 August 1698," *Calendar of State Papers Colonial*, 16:446-455.

133. "America and West Indies: September 1698, 21–25: Copy of a Letter from Governor Markham to Governor Lord Bellomont. Philadelphia, 2 September 1698," *Calendar of State Papers Colonial*, 16:446–55.

134. "America and West Indies: September 1698, 21–25: Copy of a Letter from Governor Lord Bellomont to Governor Markham. New York, 2 September 1698," *Calendar of State Papers Colonial*, 16:446–55.

135. A cocquet is a seal formerly of the English or Scottish king's customhouse.

136. "America and West Indies: August 1698, 16–20: Robert Quarry to Governor Nicholson. Philadelphia, 9 July 1698," *Calendar of State Papers Colonial*, 16:377–99; "America and West Indies: August 1698, 16–20: Robert Quarry to Governor Nicholson. Philadelphia, 21 July 1698," *Calendar of State Papers Colonial*, 16:377–99.

137. "America and West Indies: August 1698, 6–10: 733. i. Deposition of Benjamin Franks," *Calendar of State Papers Colonial*, 16:368–74.

138. "America and West Indies: August 1698, 6–10: 733. ii. Deposition of Nicholas Alderson," *Calendar of State Papers Colonial*, 16:368–74.

139. "America and West Indies: May 1700, 21–25: Examination of James How, Who Sailed from New York with Capt. Kidd, Sept. 1696," *Calendar of State Papers Colonial*, 18:263–84.

140. "America and West Indies: July 1699, 6–10: 621. Governor Lord Bellomont to the Council of Trade and Plantations," *Calendar of State Papers Colonial*, 17:327–40.

141. "America and West Indies: December 1699, 1–15: 1,034. An Account of What Captain Kidd Has Done Abroad According to the Information Received by the Commissioners for Trade and Plantations, and What Has Been Done Thereupon," *Calendar of State Papers Colonial*, 17:564–75.

142. Ibid.

143. "America and West Indies: December 1699, 1–15: 1,061. Council of Trade and Plantations to the King," *Calendar of State Papers Colonial*, 17:564–75.

144. Hanna, *Pirate Nests*, 271.

145. "America and West Indies: April 1699, 11–15: 247. William Stoughton to Mr. Secretary Vernon," *Calendar of State Papers Colonial*, 17:131–48.

146. Ibid.

147. "America and West Indies: February 1699, 21–24: 116. ix. Lord Bellomont's Reasons for Displacing Col. Thomas Willet from the Council," *Calendar of State Papers Colonial*, 17:68–79.

148. "America and West Indies: December 1701, 16–20: 1092. Council of Trade and Plantations to Governor Lord Cornbury," *Calendar of State Papers Colonial*, 19:679–91.

Chapter 5

149. "America and West Indies: March 1699, 1–10: 167. Council of Trade and Plantations to the King," *Calendar of State Papers Colonial*, 17:82–101.

150. Lydon, *Pirates*, 41; "America and West Indies: December 1696, 11–20: 517. I.T. South to the Lords Justices of Ireland. Dublin, 15 Aug. 1696," *Calendar of State Papers Colonial*, 15:248–67.

151. "America and West Indies: March 1699, 1–10: 167. Council of Trade and Plantations to the King," *Calendar of State Papers Colonial*, 17:82–101.

152. Quoted in Lydon, *Pirates*, 41.

153. "America and West Indies: March 1699, 1–10: 167. Council of Trade and Plantations to the King," *Calendar of State Papers Colonial*, 17:82–101.

154. Ibid.

155. "America and West Indies: May 1698, 16–20: 473. Governor the Earl of Bellomont to Council of Trade and Plantations," *Calendar of State Papers Colonial*, 16:217–34.

156. "America and West Indies: March 1699, 1–10: 167. Council of Trade and Plantations to the King," *Calendar of State Papers Colonial*, 17:82–101.

157. Lydon, *Pirates*, 50–51.

158. Ibid., 51–54.

159. Ibid., 54–55.

160. "America and West Indies: May 1699, 1–5: 343. Governor the Earl of Bellomont to Council of Trade and Plantations," *Calendar of State Papers Colonial*, 17:181–96.

161. "America and West Indies: June 1699, 12–20: 530. i. Governor Blakiston to Mr. Secretary Vernon," *Calendar of State Papers Colonial*, 17:283–91.

162. "America and West Indies: June 1699, 1–10: 483. Col. Quary to the Council of Trade and Plantations," *Calendar of State Papers Colonial*, 17:266–83.

163. "America and West Indies: June 1699, 1–10: 495. Col. Quary to the Council of Trade and Plantations," *Calendar of State Papers Colonial*, 17:266–83.

164. Also spelled "Graverard."

165. "America and West Indies: June 1699, 1–10: 495. Col. Quary to the Council of Trade and Plantations," *Calendar of State Papers Colonial*, 17:266–83.

166. A Rix dollar is any of the various old dollar coins of Germany, the Netherlands or Scandinavia and was used in most Dutch colonies throughout seventeenth-century America.

167. "America and West Indies: June 1699, 1–10: 495. Col. Quary to the Council of Trade and Plantations," *Calendar of State Papers Colonial*, 17:266–83.

168. A hundredweight (abbreviated as cwt) is a standard unit of weight or mass used in certain commodities trading contracts. In North America, a hundredweight is equal to 100 pounds; in the United Kingdom, a hundredweight is 112 pounds.

169. A Lyon dollar was a Dutch coin of the seventeenth century that featured a lion on both sides. It was small on one side with a shield and was large on the other.

170. "America and West Indies: June 1699, 1–10: 512. ii. Giles Shelley to Mr. Delencie, or, in His Absence, Mr. John Barbarie in New York," *Calendar of State Papers Colonial*, 17:266–83.

171. "America and West Indies: August 1699, 21–25: 740. Governor the Earl of Bellomont to the Council of Trade and Plantations," *Calendar of State Papers Colonial*, 17:395–412.

Chapter 6

172. "America and West Indies: August 1699, 28–31: 746. Governor the Earl of Bellomont to the Council of Trade and Plantations," *Calendar of State Papers Colonial*, 17:412–20.

173. Ibid.

174. "America and West Indies: August 1699, 28–31: 746. xix. Boston, Sep. 4, 1699. Deposition of Captain Kidd," *Calendar of State Papers Colonial*, 17:412–20.

175. "America and West Indies: October 1699, 16–20: L.G. of New York to Lord Bellomont. Oct. 23, 1699," *Calendar of State Papers Colonial*, 17:463–82.

176. "America and West Indies: October 1699, 16–20: 878. vii. Paroculus Parmyter to Lord Bellomont," *Calendar of State Papers Colonial*, 17:463–82.

177. "America and West Indies: August 1699, 7–10: 704. Minutes of Council of New York," *Calendar of State Papers Colonial*, 17:385–88.

178. "America and West Indies: August 1699, 21–25: 740. Governor the Earl of Bellomont to the Council of Trade and Plantations," *Calendar of State Papers Colonial*, 17:395–412.

179. "America and West Indies: August 1699, 21–25: 740. xiv. Copy of a Letter from Gov. Bass to the L.G. of New York, Burlington, May 30, 1699," *Calendar of State Papers Colonial*, 17:395–412.

180. "America and West Indies: November 1699, 27–30: 1,011. Governor the Earl of Bellomont to the Council of Trade and Plantations," *Calendar of State Papers Colonial*, 17:542–64.

181. "America and West Indies: February 1700, 11–15: 113. Petition of Jeremiah Basse, Esq. and John Lofting, Merchant, to the House of Commons," *Calendar of State Papers Colonial*, 18:64–73.

182. "America and West Indies: December 1700, 6–10: 983. Governor the Earl of Bellomont to Mr. Secretary Vernon," *Calendar of State Papers Colonial*, 18:716–31.

183. "America and West Indies: April 1700, 26–30: 366. William Penn to the Council of Trade and Plantations," *Calendar of State Papers Colonial*, 18:206–17; Morgan, *Pirates & Patriots*, 15.

184. "America and West Indies: April 1700, 26–30: 366. William Penn to the Council of Trade and Plantations," *Calendar of State Papers Colonial*, 18:206–17.

185. "America and West Indies: June 1700, 1–5: 500. Col. Quary to the Council of Trade and Plantations," *Calendar of State Papers Colonial*, 18:296–302.

186. "America and West Indies: December 1701, 2–5: 1054. Geo. Larkin to the Council of Trade and Plantations," *Calendar of State Papers Colonial*, 19:630–59.

187. Hanna, *Pirate Nests*, 310–11.

188. Burrows and Wallace, *Gotham*, 121.

Chapter 7

189. Donnelly and Diehl, *Pirates of New Jersey*, 25–29; Peterson, *Patriots, Pirates, & Pineys*, 21–22.

190. Johnson, *General History*, 82; Donnelly and Diehl, *Pirates of New Jersey*, 25–29.

191. Johnson, *General History*, 82.

192. Donnelly and Diehl, *Pirates of New Jersey*, 37–38.

193. "America and West Indies: June 1723: 606. Governor Burnet to Lord Carteret," *Calendar of State Papers Colonial*, 33:282–301.

194. Kyriakodis, *Lost Waterfront*, 137.

195. Dolin, *Black Flags, Blue Waters*, 260–61.

196. Ibid., 270–71.

Chapter 8

197. Burrows and Wallace, *Gotham*, 169.

198. Ibid.

199. Ibid., 169, 182.

200. Ibid., 183.

201. Ibid.

202. Ibid., 184.

Chapter 9

203. Shomette, *Privateers of the Revolution*, 16.

204. Ibid., 247.

205. Shomette, *Privateers of the Revolution*, 17.

206. Quoted in Shomette, *Privateers of the Revolution*, 17.

207. Shomette, *Privateers of the Revolution*, 21–22.

208. Morgan, *Pirates & Patriots*, 26.

209. *Materiel* refers to military materials and equipment.

210. Morgan, *Pirates & Patriots*, 26–27.
211. Ibid., 27–28.

Chapter 10

212. Library of Congress, Rare Book and Special Collections Division, "In Congress, Wednesday."
213. State Archives of North Carolina, "Letter of Marque."
214. Hand and Stites, *Cape May Navy*, 27.
215. Three Decks' Forum, "*Galatea* (1776)."
216. Donnelly and Diehl, *Pirates of New Jersey*, 49–50.
217. Ibid., 50–51.
218. Pierce, *Smugglers' Woods*, 54.
219. "New-Jersey, March 20th," *Documents Relating to the Revolutionary History*, 4:246.
220. "New-Jersey, April 22," *Documents Relating to the Revolutionary History*, 4:338; Donnelly and Diehl, *Pirates of New Jersey*, 51–53 Hand and Stites, *Cape May Navy*, 10.
221. Hand and Stites, *Cape May Navy*, 10.
222. Pierce, *Smugglers' Woods*, 54; Donnelly and Diehl, *Pirates of New Jersey*, 52–54.
223. Hand and Stites, *Cape May Navy*, 10.
224. Ibid., 19–20.
225. Ibid., 19–24.
226. *Mutton* refers to the flesh of a sheep, particularly a mature sheep.
227. Quoted in Hand and Stites, *Cape May Navy*, 30.

Chapter 11

228. Quoted in Hand and Stites, *Cape May Navy*, 33.
229. "Lucy Knox to Henry Knox, March 18, 1777," Gilder Lehrman Collection GLC02437.00553.
230. Hand and Stites, *Cape May Navy*, 27–28.
231. Foy, "Royal Navy's Employment," 6–35.
232. Winch, *Gentleman of Color*, 45–46.

Chapter 12

233. Hanna, "What Is Known About Pirates."
234. Quoted in Johnson, *General History*, 37.

BIBLIOGRAPHY

Books

Burrows, Edwin G., and Mike Wallace. *Gotham: A History of New York City to 1898.* New York: Oxford University Press, 1999.

Dolin, Eric Jay. *Black Flags, Blue Waters: The Epic History of America's Most Notorious Pirates.* New York: Liveright Publishing, 2018.

Donnelly, Mark P., and Daniel Diehl. *Pirates of New Jersey: Plunder and High Adventure on the Garden State Coastline.* Mechanicsburg, PA: Stackpole Books, 2010.

Hand, J.P., and Daniel Stites. *The Cape May Navy: Delaware Bay Privateers in the American Revolution.* Charleston, SC: The History Press, 2018.

Hanna, Mark. *Pirate Nests and the Rise of the British Empire, 1570–1740.* Chapel Hill: University of North Carolina Press, 2015.

Kyriakodis, Harry. *Philadelphia's Lost Waterfront.* Charleston, SC: The History Press, 2011.

Lydon, James G. *Pirates, Privateers, and Profits.* Upper Saddle River, NJ: Gregg Press, 1970.

Morgan, Michael. *Pirates & Patriots: Tales of the Delaware Coast.* New York: Algora Publishing, 2005.

Peterson, Robert A. *Patriots, Pirates, & Pineys: Sixty Who Shaped New Jersey.* Medford, NJ: Plexus Publishing Inc., 1998.

Pierce, Arthur Dudley. *Smugglers' Woods: Jaunts and Journeys in Colonial and Revolutionary New Jersey.* New Brunswick, NJ: Rutgers University Press, 1960.

Rediker, Marcus. *Between the Devil and the Deep Blue Sea: Merchant Seamen, Pirates, and the Anglo-American Maritime World, 1700–1750.* New York: Cambridge University Press, 1987.

Ritchie, Robert C. *Captain Kidd and the War Against the Pirates.* Cambridge, MA: Harvard University Press, 1986.

Rogoziński, Jan. *Honor Among Thieves: Captain Kidd, Henry Avery, and the Pirate Democracy in the Indian Ocean.* Mechanicsburg, PA: Stackpole Books, 2000.

Shomette, Donald Grady. *Privateers of the Revolution: War on the New Jersey Coast, 1775–1783.* Atglen, PA: Schiffer Publishing Ltd., 2016.

Winch, Julie. *A Gentleman of Color: The Life of James Forten.* New York: Oxford University Press, 2002.

Journal Articles

Foy, Charles R. "The Royal Navy's Employment of Black Mariners and Maritime Workers, 1754–1783." *International Maritime History Journal* 28, no. 1 (February 2016): 6–35.

Hanna, Mark G. "A Lot of What Is Known About Pirates Is Not True, and a Lot of What Is True Is Not Known." *Humanities* 38, no. 1 (Winter 2017). www.neh.gov.

Judd, Jacob. "Frederick Philipse and the Madagascar Trade." *New York Historical Society Quarterly* 55, no. 4 (1971): 354–74.

Published Primary Sources

"America and West Indies." In *Calendar of State Papers Colonial, America and West Indies: Volumes 1–41, 1574–1739.* Edited by W. Noel Sainsbury and J.W. Fortescue. London: Her Majesty's Stationery Office, 1896. www.british-history.ac.uk.

Fox, E.T. *Pirates in Their Own Words.* United Kingdom: Lulu.com, 2014.

Johnson, Captain Charles. *A General History of the Pyrates.* Salt Lake City, UT: Project Gutenberg, 2012. www.gutenberg.org.

Library of Congress, Rare Book and Special Collections Division. "In Congress, Wednesday. April 3, 1776: Instructions to the Commanders of Private Ships or Vessels of War, Which Shall Have Commissions or Letters of Marque and Reprisal, Authorising Them to Make Captures of British Vessels and Cargoes." Documents from the Continental Congress and the Constitutional Convention, 1774 to 1789. www.lccn.loc.gov.

State Archives of North Carolina. "Letter of Marque Signed by John Hancock, 1776." Vault Collection. www.digital.ncdcr.gov.

"State of New-Jersey, April 22, 1780: To Be Sold." In *Documents Relating to the Revolutionary History: State of New Jersey.* Vol. 4. Edited by William Nelson. Trenton, NJ: State Gazette Publishing Co., 1914.

"State of New-Jersey, March 20th, 1780: TO BE SOLD." In *Documents Relating to the Revolutionary History: State of New Jersey.* Vol. 4. Edited by William Nelson. Trenton, NJ: State Gazette Publishing Co., 1914.

"The Substance of the Examinations of John Brown &c., 6 May 1717." Printed as an appendix of *The Trials of Eight Persons Indicted for Piracy.* Boston, MA: Printed by B. Green for John Edwards and sold at his shop in King's Street, 1718.

"Volume 54: June 21–July 14, 1698: 45. Letter of Lord Bellomont to the Lords [of the Treasury]." In *Calendar of Treasury Papers, Volume 2, 1697–1702*. Edited by Joseph Redington. London: Her Majesty's Stationery Office, 1871, 172–83. www.british-history.ac.uk.

Archival Sources

"The Case of Samuell Burgess." SP 34/36, f. 35.
"Deposition of Adam Baldridge, 5 May 1699." CO 5/1042, no. 30ii.
"The Examination of Richard Roper, 27 August 1701." HCA 1.53, ff. 100–101.
"A List of the Prices that Capt. Jacobs Sold Licquors and Other Goods att St. Mary's, 9 June 1698." HCA 1/98, f. 142.
"Lucy Knox to Henry Knox, March 18, 1777." Gilder Lehrman Collection GLC02437.00553.
"Penn to BOT, Philadelphia, April 28, 1700." CO 5/1260, no. 43.
"Weaver's Reply." CO 391/11, f. 215–16.

Web Sources

Three Decks' Forum. "British Sixth Rate Ship, *Galatea* (1776)." www.threedecks.org.

INDEX

ABOUT THE AUTHOR

J amie L.H. Goodall, PhD, is a staff historian at the U.S. Army Center of Military History in Washington, D.C. She also teaches undergraduate history courses for Southern New Hampshire University's online program. Jamie has a PhD in history from the Ohio State University, with specializations in Atlantic world, early American and military histories. She is also a first-generation college student. Her publications include, "Tippling Houses, Rum Shops, & Taverns: How Alcohol Fueled Informal Commercial Networks and Knowledge Exchange in the West Indies" in the *Journal of Maritime History, Pirates of the Chesapeake Bay: From the Colonial Era to the Oyster Wars* from The History Press (2020) and *Pirates: Shipwrecks, Conquests, and Their Lasting Legacy* for National Geographic (2021). She lives in northern Virginia with her partner, Kyle, and two boxer dogs, Thomas Jefferson "T.J." and John Tyler "J.T." Her passions include tattoos, history, teaching, true crime, sunshine, the ocean and—of course—pirates. She also considers herself a connoisseur of the three Bs: books, booze and beaches! When not writing, you can usually find her on Twitter: @L_ Historienne.

CPSIA information can be obtained
at www.ICGtesting.com
Printed in the USA
LVHW080853190622
721603LV00004B/209